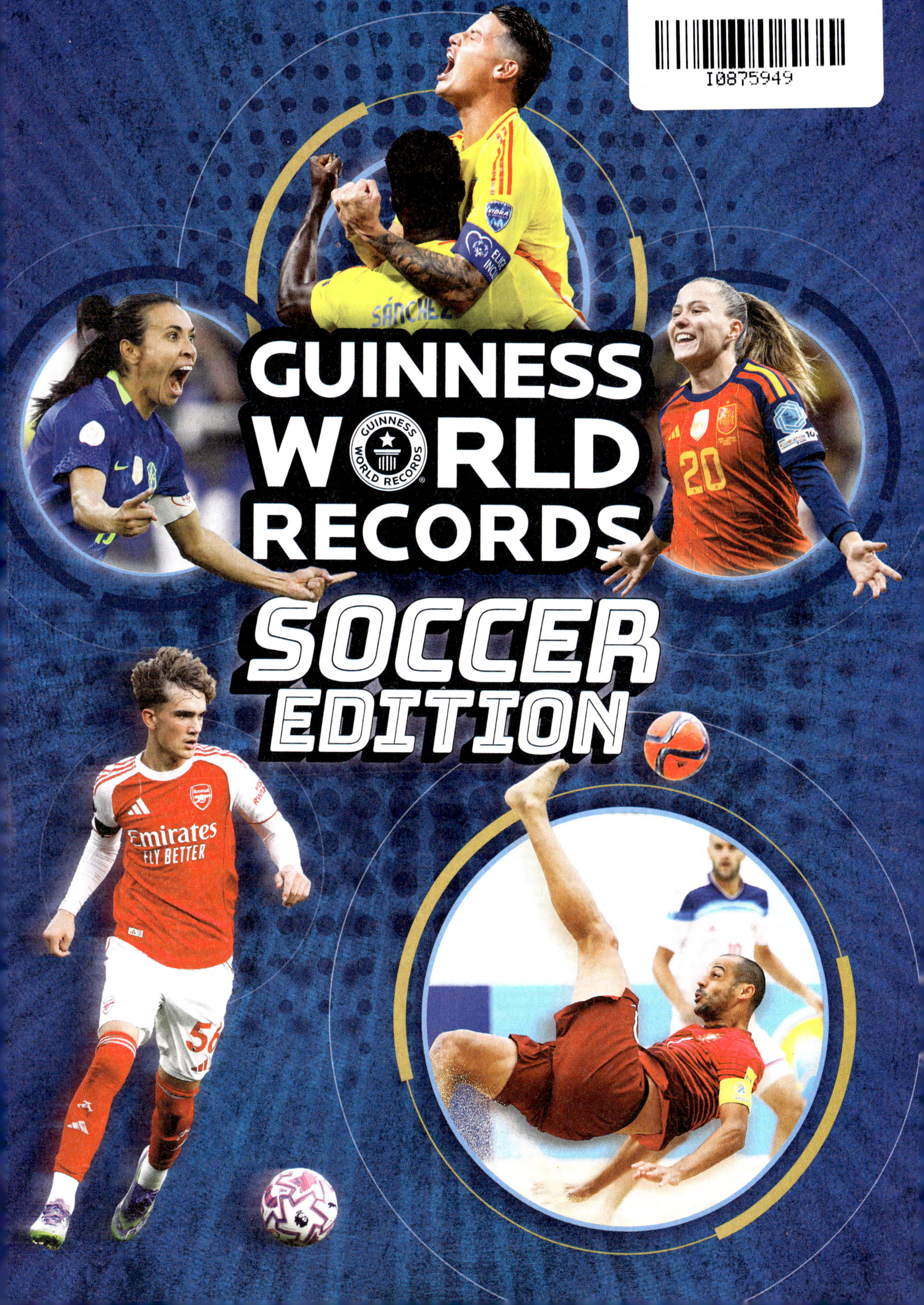

GUINNESS WORLD RECORDS

SOCCER EDITION

FOOTBALL EDITION 2027

SVP Brand Strategy & Global Publishing
Nadine Causey
Editor-in-Chief
Craig Glenday
Publishing Director
Jane Boatfield
Senior Editor, Football Edition
Tom Beckerlegge
Senior Picture Editor
Abby Taylor
Picture Editors
Alice Jessop, Saffron Fradley
Senior Managing Editor
Adam Millward
Senior Editors
Alice Bell, Ben Hollingum
Editor
Caitlin Hyem
Proofreading & Fact-Checking
Matthew White
Layout & Cover Design
Paul Wylie-Deacon and Richard Page at 55design.co.uk
Indexer
Tim Appleton
VP Global Production & Supply Chain
Patricia Magill
Production & Distribution Manager
Thomas McCurdy
Senior Talent Researcher
Charlie Anderson
Production Consultants
Yannick Laag, Astrid Renders, Kevin Sarney, Julia Seebach, Dennis Thon
Printing & Binding
Mohn Media Mohndruck GmbH, Gütersloh, Germany
Global Marketing Director
Nicholas Brookes
Senior Content Manager
Eleonora Pilastro
Senior Marketing Executive
Nicole Dyer-Rainford
CRM Marketing Manager: Jody Ho
Head of Global Brand Communications
Amber-Georgina Maskell
Senior PR Manager
Anna Hammersley
PR Manager
Madalyn Bielfeld
Global Sales Director
Joel Smith
Senior Key Account Manager
Mavis Sarfo
International Sales Manager
Alexandra Bielikova
Director of Brand Strategy
Lucy Hunter
Head of Brand Management
Juliet Dawson
Brand Manager
Jack Brockbank
Head of Design
Rebecca Fisher
Senior Designer
Kelsey Bell
Designer
Aaron Quinn
Reprographics
Resmiye Kahraman and Louise Pinnock at BORN Group

British Library Cataloguing-in-publication data: a catalogue record for this book is available from the British Library

UK: 978-1-80650-024-6
US: 978-1-80650-027-7
CAN: 978-1-80650-034-5
AUS: 978-1-80650-037-6

Records are made to be broken – indeed, it is one of the key criteria for a record category – so if you find a record that you think you can beat, tell us about it by making a record claim. Always contact us before making a record attempt.

Sustainability
At Guinness World Records, we continue to run our business in the most sustainable, environmentally conscious way we can. We are committed to ethical and responsible sourcing of paper, as well as ink, and we work to ensure that all our supply-chain partners meet the highest international standards for sustainable production and energy management. For more information, please contact us.

The paper used in this publication is produced by UPM Communication Papers and comes from the UPM Rauma paper mill in Finland.

UPM Communication Papers is a leading global producer of graphic papers, embracing sustainability and high environmental performance. UPM is committed to climate action through climate-positive forestry practices, emission reductions throughout the value chain, and scientifically verifying the climate impact of its products.

UPM is the only paper and forest company recognized in the Dow Jones World and European Sustainability Indices, underscoring its commitment to sustainable practices.

GWR has a very thorough accreditation system for records verification. However, while every effort is made to ensure accuracy, GWR cannot be held responsible for any errors contained in this work. Feedback from our readers on any point of accuracy is always welcomed.

GWR uses metric and imperial measurements. Exceptions are made for some scientific data where metric measurements are universally accepted, and some sports data. Where a specific date is given, the exchange rate is calculated according to the currency values at the time. Where only a year date is given, the exchange rate is calculated from 31 Dec of that year.

Appropriate advice should always be taken when attempting to break or set records. Participants undertake records entirely at their own risk. GWR has complete discretion over whether or not to include a record attempt in any of its publications. Being a GWR record holder does not guarantee you a place in any Guinness World Records publication.

Printed in Germany by Mohn Media
Guinness World Records Limited's authorized representative in the European Union is Mohn Media Mohndruck GmbH, Carl-Bertelsmann-Straße 161M, 33311 Gütersloh, Germany
www.mohnmedia.de

Registered address:
Ground Floor,
The Rookery, 2 Dyott Street,
London, WC1A 1DE

THE JIM PATTISON GROUP

OFFICIALLY AMAZING

FOREWORD

DANIEL CUTTING

CUTTING EDGE

Daniel (above with GWR's Mark McKinley) currently holds four record titles:

Most football touches with the lips in one minute: 153

Greatest height to flick and control a football with the neck: 6 m (19 ft 8 in)

Longest time to control a football on the chest: 44.57 sec

Fastest 100 m run with a football balanced on the head: 18.53 sec

Hi! I'm Daniel, freestyle footballer and world record holder. It's my honour to welcome you to the *Guinness World Records Football Edition 2027*! I really enjoyed last year's book, so it's great to see it back again.

When I was younger, I absolutely loved reading the *Guinness World Records* annuals. Becoming a world record holder was always something I dreamed of – it was inspiring to believe that one day I could be the best in the world at something. I went on to achieve multiple GWR titles, and it's been an incredible journey.

I fell in love with football at a very young age – as soon as I could walk, there was a ball put in front of me! I started playing regularly and joined local teams. Freestyling gave me the opportunity to express myself and be creative with the ball, pushing boundaries by trying things that hadn't been done before. In 2011, I achieved three world records on the same day at an event held at my local football club, MK Dons. Attempting multiple titles required really intensive training, but this only made the experience even more rewarding and memorable – especially when I knew that I had got them all!

As a lifelong Arsenal fan, I was made up to see Gunners and England captain Declan Rice on the cover of this year's *Football Edition*. You'll also find him on p.68, for his heroics against Real Madrid in the UEFA Champions League. I also love that Max Dowman (p.12) has made it into the Class of '27, alongside some of the best young record breakers in the game.

My biggest football inspirations growing up were Ronaldinho and David Beckham. Ronaldinho had everything – skill, creativity, flair. Most importantly, you could see how much he loved playing; the joy and freedom in his style. Beckham was incredibly talented, but it was his work ethic that had the biggest impact on me. He was known for arriving early at training and staying behind to practise his free kicks. I realized that natural ability alone isn't enough – you have to put in the work to be the best.

One of my favourite football memories is Beckham's last-gasp free kick against Greece, which earned England qualification to the 2002 FIFA World Cup. I've been lucky enough to attend several World Cup tournaments, getting the chance to experience not only the football but also the different cultures. You'll find all the best records from the 2026 FIFA World Cup on pp.120–23, and check out the World Cup Classics section for in-depth analysis of some of the competition's best-ever games (pp.134–57).

Whether it's as a freestyler, a fan or a content creator, I've lost none of my passion for the game, and it's something I've passed on to my own son.

I know how hard the team at GWR have been working on this book – I hope you enjoy reading it!

Daniel

CONTENTS

Trace the history of the world's most expensive footballer – from £1,000 to €222 m!

A comprehensive round-up of the best records arranged by leagues and tournaments

Welcome to the *Guinness World Records Football Edition 2027*! Our records team has been hard at work in the last 12 months, collating and updating the very best in soccer superlatives. Whichever team you support and whomever your favourite players are, you'll find all the facts and stats you need inside these pages...

The GWR Football Edition celebrates the best of the men's and the women's game from leagues across the world.

Get the tactical lowdown on the 20 greatest FIFA World Cup matches

CONTINENTAL INTERNATIONAL TOURNAMENTS

WORLD TOURNAMENTS

WORLD CUP CLASSICS

FEATURES

EXTRA TIME

EDITOR'S LETTER

Welcome to the *Guinness World Records Football Edition 2027*! Following the success of our first-ever edition last year, we're back with a vengeance, with a host of new features and updated records from both the men's and women's game.

It's been another incredible year for football, with amazing tournaments engrossing audiences and exciting new talent coming through. This means only one thing... more records! We've been able to present GWR certificates to stars from around the world, including (*left, from top*) Erling Haaland, Yu Kobayashi and Maria McAneny. Given everything that these players have achieved on the pitch, it's been an honour to see what becoming a record holder means to them.

This year, we're breaking down our records on a tournament-by-tournament basis – from some of the world's biggest national leagues, like the English Premier League and La Liga, to continental and world competitions. These are headlined – of course – by the 2026 FIFA World Cup, the largest in the history of the competition. We're delighted to bring you all the latest records from the tournament, hot off the presses!

We're also introducing the Class of '27, a list of the hottest young footballing stars. While some of our record breakers will be familiar to you, others you'll be meeting for the first time – but if you hadn't heard of them yet, you soon will do! Elsewhere, we take a deep dive

Arsenal's Max Dowman is the youngest member of our super-talented Class of '27 – turn to p.10 to see the full list.

GLOBAL GAME

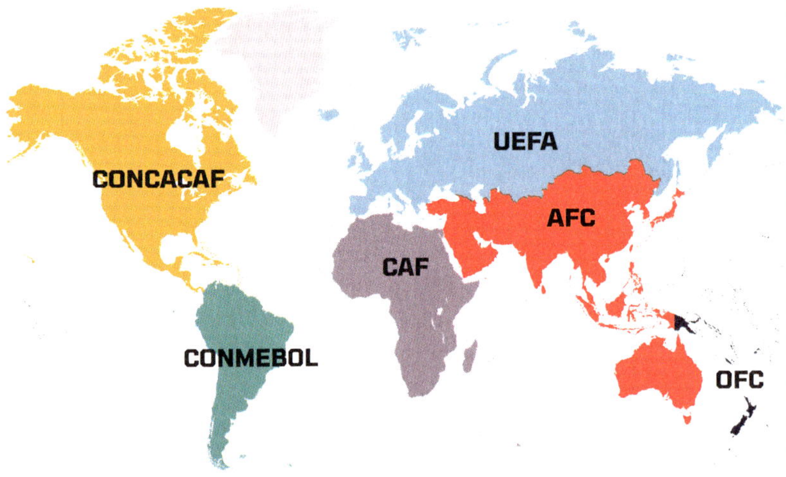

Throughout this book, you'll find references to the six confederations that operate under the umbrella of FIFA, the global footballing body. They cover six of Earth's seven continents, with only Antarctica remaining a football-free zone.

into the history of the world's **most expensive football player**, and bring you our list of the 20 best FIFA World Cup games. There are stand-alone features throughout the *GWR Football Edition*, taking a sideways look at the beautiful game. Check out some of the most unusual pitches on the planet, and find out which famous people made the grade to join our Celebrity Soccer XI.

One feature making a welcome return is our Extra Time section at the back of the book, complete with the best freestyle records from the past 12 months and starring the talented brothers James and Ben Taylor. Freestyle world champion Isabel Wilkins is back to explain how YOU can earn your own Guinness World Records title, and to round things off there's a brain-busting football quiz.

Right, that's enough from me: the players are in the tunnel and it's time for you to get stuck in!

Tom Beckerlegge
GWR Football Edition Editor

LARGEST FOOTBALL

On 12 Jun 2026, a supersized soccer ball with a diameter of 14.6 m (47 ft 11 in) was unveiled in Boston, Massachusetts, USA. Commissioned by Massachusetts Port Authority, Suffolk Construction and HNTB Corporation (all USA), it was created to celebrate Boston's role as a host city for the 2026 FIFA World Cup.

Napoli and Argentina legend Diego Maradona makes two appearances in our Transfer Record Timeline on pp.84–93.

Champions Spain feature heavily in our rundown of the best records from the 2026 FIFA World Cup. Join the party on pp.120–23.

YEAR IN FOOTBALL

With big games coming thick and fast throughout the year, it was no surprise that 2025/26 saw a slew of footballing records fall. And so – naturally – Guinness World Records was in the thick of the action...

LIGHTNING STRIKE

On 25 Mar 2026, Guinness World Records Editor-in-Chief Craig Glenday presented Celtic Women striker Maria McAneny with her record certificate for the **fastest goal in women's football**. McAneny scored from the centre circle after just 4.1 sec of Celtic's Scottish Women's Premier League tie against Hibernian on 21 Dec 2025. "It was just a spur-of-the-moment thing," McAneny said of her goal, "and thankfully it went in! It's a great feeling – definitely not an achievement I ever thought I'd have."

Sarina Wiegman (NLD) extended her record for the **most wins of The Best FIFA Women's Coach award**, picking up her fifth trophy on 16 Dec 2025. The England coach steered the Lionesses to back-to-back wins of the UEFA Women's Euros (*see p.111*).

"This record is a reminder that football truly belongs to everyone," FIFA President Gianni Infantino posted on Instagram.

TEAM OF NATIONS

On 5 Nov 2025, the FIFA Member Associations Division came together to achieve the GWR title for the **most nationalities in a football exhibition match**. A total of 68 countries from across the globe were represented, ranging from Azerbaijan to Zimbabwe. The game took place at the Mohammed VI Football Academy in Salé, Morocco, and lasted almost 3 hr, with players having to participate for at least 10 min in order to qualify. GWR Adjudicator Joanne Brent was on hand to run the rule over the multinational match.

TROPHY TREBLE

The Ballon d'Or is an annual award by *France Football* magazine to the players voted the best in the game. At the 2025 ceremony, Spain and Barcelona star Aitana Bonmatí claimed the outright record for the **most wins of the Women's Ballon d'Or**, earning the trophy for the third consecutive year. Ousmane Dembélé took the men's award, his goals having powered Paris Saint-Germain to a continental treble.

SPANISH KINGS

On 18 Apr 2026, Real Sociedad secured their fourth Copa del Rey on penalties after a 2–2 draw with Atlético Madrid. The Basque side got off to a flying start, Ander Barrenetxea (ESP) netting the **fastest goal in a Copa del Rey final** after just 14 sec. The Spain international celebrated his GWR certificate with his teammates (*left*).

Q&A: JUSTIN KLUIVERT

On 13 Sep 2025, AFC Bournemouth striker Justin Kluivert (NLD) was presented with his GWR certificate for the **most penalties converted in an EPL match** – three, against Wolverhampton Wanderers on 30 Nov 2024. We put the ice-cool finisher on the spot with some questions about his penalty prowess.

Have you ever taken three penalties before in a game?
Never. I actually used to be scared to take penalties!

How often do you practise penalties? Do you have a specific routine that you go through?
I always practise the day before the game. I like to wait and see where the keeper goes and then shoot the other side.

How did it feel when you scored the third penalty? Did you know that you'd set a new record?
I didn't know but I was super-happy. Scoring a hat-trick is a memory you will never forget, because you get to take the ball home.

Not only did you score all three spot-kicks, but your teammate Evanilson was the player fouled each time! Did he ask to take any of the penalties?
No, because he trusts me!

You've played across Europe, famously becoming only the third player ever to score in all of the top 5 leagues. Who is the best penalty taker you've seen?
Mario Balotelli.

Did you know that your father [former Ajax striker Patrick] also has a GWR record, as the youngest goal scorer in a UEFA Champions League final?
I didn't know that he had one, but our certificates will have to go up next to each other!

What advice do you have for young players hoping to hone their skills from 12 yards out?
Don't think twice when you're about to take it.

How does it feel to be a GWR title holder?
Beautiful!

CLASS OF '27

Welcome to the Class of '27 – our selection of some of the world's finest players aged 27 or under, all of whom have at one time held or contributed to a GWR record title. Our line-up is arranged by age, from youngest to oldest, and includes not only today's superstars, but also the brightest talents of tomorrow.

CONTENTS

CHELSEA
USA
20
QATAR
AIRWAYS

CLASS OF '27

MAX DOWMAN

Having trained with the Arsenal first team since the age of 14, Max Dowman has long been tipped for great things – and in 2025/26, he showed why. A skilful winger, he loves to take on opponents and draw fouls in key positions. He came on against Leeds United on 23 Aug 2025 to become the second-youngest player in EPL history, winning his side a penalty. Dowman went on to break major records in both the EPL and the UEFA Champions League, and he's only just getting started...

YOUNGEST PLAYER IN THE UEFA CHAMPIONS LEAGUE

Dowman (b. 31 Dec 2009) was 15 years 308 days old when he came on as a second-half substitute for Arsenal against Slavia Praha on 4 Nov 2025. The Gunners won the away tie 3–0. Dowman became the first 15-year-old Champions League player, breaking the previous record of Borussia Dortmund's Youssoufa Moukoko by 75 days.

Dowman takes the plaudits from the Arsenal faithful after becoming the **youngest goal scorer in the EPL**, against Everton on 14 Mar 2026 (*see pp.48–49*).

CLASS OF '27

CAVAN SULLIVAN

On 17 Jul 2024, Cavan Sullivan (b. 28 Sep 2009) made US sporting history when he took to the field for the Philadelphia Union against the New England Revolution. Aged 14 years 293 days, he became not only the **youngest MLS player**, but the youngest player in any North American major-league sport. Expectations around the midfielder grow as Sullivan develops, making his first MLS start in 2025. He has signed an agreement with EPL powerhouses Manchester City that will see him make a transatlantic move when he turns 18.

Sullivan scored his first two senior goals against Trinidad & Tobago's Defence Force in the CONCACAF Champions Cup on 26 Feb 2026.

YOUTH LEADER

Sullivan was the youngest member of the US team at the 2025 FIFA U-17 World Cup in Qatar. He scored the winner against Burkina Faso before converting a Panenka penalty against Tajikistan. His performance against Czechia in the final group game earned him the Player of the Match award.

CLASS OF '27

GILBERTO MORA

Mexico's next big thing has enjoyed a startling rise to the top of the game. Gilberto Mora was just 15 when he made his league debut for Club Tijuana on 19 Aug 2024. Two weeks later, on his first start for the club, the midfielder became the **youngest goal scorer in Liga MX** (*see below*). His age might raise eyebrows, but Mora has impressed his coaches with his maturity and focus. He made his Mexico debut at the 2025 CONCACAF Gold Cup, where he broke a record set by none other than Lamine Yamal.

YOUNGEST WINNER OF A FIFA MEN'S INTERNATIONAL TOURNAMENT
Mora (b. 14 Oct 2008) was 16 years 265 days old when he helped Mexico beat the USA in the final of the 2025 CONCACAF Gold Cup. It was only Mora's third international game, having made his debut in the quarter-finals. He beat the previous record of Lamine Yamal, who won the 2024 UEFA Euros with Spain the day after his 17th birthday.

On 31 Aug 2024, Mora became the **youngest goal scorer in Liga MX**, netting during Club Tijuana's 2–1 win over Club León aged 15 years 322 days.

CLASS OF '27

FRANCESCO CAMARDA

Francesco Camarda built a fearsome reputation during his youth career, reportedly scoring almost 500 goals for AC Milan's academy. When the club was hit by an injury crisis in the run-up to a game against Fiorentina on 25 Nov 2023, they turned to their precocious striker. Camarda (ITA, b. 10 Mar 2008) became the **youngest player in Serie A**, aged 15 years 260 days. Milan had to seek special dispensation from the Italian Football Federation to field a player under 16. In 2025, Camarda was sent on loan to Lecce, and he wasted no time in making his mark.

Camarda was called up to the Italy U-21 squad in Oct 2025. He scored three goals in his first two games, against Sweden and Armenia.

LION OF LECCE

On 28 Sep 2025, Camarda scored his first goal in Serie A, heading home from a corner to earn Lecce a point in their 2–2 draw with Bologna. Aged 17 years 202 days, he became Lecce's youngest scorer in the Italian top flight. The club had an option to buy Camarda when his loan deal expired.

CLASS OF '27

JORTHY MOKIO

One of the most sought-after defensive talents in world football, Jorthy Mokio can play either at the back or in midfield. Born in Belgium, he came through the ranks at Gent and made just four appearances before signing for Dutch heavyweights Ajax – having reportedly turned down offers from some of Europe's biggest clubs. Mokio made his debut in the UEFA Europa League on 29 Aug 2024, becoming Ajax's youngest-ever non-Dutch player. And he would set another record in the same competition before the season was out (*see below*).

Mokio made his debut for Belgium against Ukraine on 20 Mar 2025. Aged 17 years 20 days, he was the second-youngest player ever in the UEFA Nations League, after Estonia's Patrik Kristal (*see p.100*).

YOUNGEST GOAL SCORER IN A UEFA EUROPA LEAGUE KNOCKOUT MATCH

On 13 Feb 2025, Mokio (b. 29 Feb 2008) volleyed home for Ajax against Union Saint-Gilloise at the age of 16 years 350 days. The Dutch side ran out 2–0 winners in their first-leg play-off. Mokio became the third-youngest scorer outright in the UEFA Europa League, behind Romelu Lukaku (16 years 218 days) and Iker Muniain (16 years 272 days).

HAINE EAMES

The 2024/25 season was a breakout year for Haine Eames of the Central Coast Mariners, who has quickly become the talk of Australian football. On just his sixth appearance, 16-year-old Eames found the net in a 1–1 draw with Macarthur to become one of the A-League's youngest-ever scorers (*see below*). He also made the step up to the AFC Champions League Elite, taking on some of Asia's biggest names. Eames's leadership abilities are rare for such a young player and have attracted interest from European clubs. A-League fans should enjoy him while they can...

YOUNGEST CAPTAIN IN THE AFC CHAMPIONS LEAGUE ELITE

On 18 Feb 2025, Eames (b. 27 Feb 2008) donned the captain's armband during Central Coast Mariners' tie against Kawasaki Frontale at the age of 16 years 357 days. He led a fresh-faced line-up whose starting XI had an average age of just 21. However, the teenage skipper couldn't prevent the Mariners sinking to a 2–0 defeat in Kawasaki, Japan.

Youngest goal scorers in A-League Men

PLAYER	TEAM	DATE	AGE
Mohamed Touré	Adelaide United	14 Feb 2020	15 years 325 days
Nestory Irankunda	Adelaide United	30 Jan 2022	15 years 355 days
Archie Goodwin	Newcastle Jets	10 Jun 2021	16 years 215 days
Luke Brooke-Smith	Wellington Phoenix	22 Feb 2025	16 years 261 days
Haine Eames	Central Coast Mariners	23 Dec 2024	16 years 300 days

LENNART KARL

One of the breakout stars of the 2025/26 season, Lennart Karl has earned comparisons with none other than Lionel Messi. He made his debut for Bayern Munich at the 2025 FIFA Club World Cup. A diminutive left-footer with excellent close control and darting changes of direction, Karl has a flair for long-range strikes. He scored on his first UEFA Champions League start, and his first Bundesliga goal – a strike from outside the box against Borussia Mönchengladbach on 25 Oct 2025 – earned him the Goal of the Month award. Karl received a call-up to the national side in Mar 2026, coming on during Germany's 4–3 win over Switzerland.

YOUNGEST PLAYER TO SCORE IN THREE CONSECUTIVE UEFA CHAMPIONS LEAGUE APPEARANCES

Karl (b. 22 Feb 2008) was 17 years 290 days old when he scored against Sporting CP on 9 Dec 2025 to complete three Champions League matches in a row with a goal. He had also struck against Club Brugge and Arsenal. Karl took the record from Kylian Mbappé, who scored his third goal in three games for Monaco aged 18 years 113 days in Apr 2017.

In 2018, aged 10, Karl went viral with an audacious goal he scored for Eintracht Frankfurt. He brought down a high ball with a backheel flick, before spinning and volleying it in with the same foot.

KONSTANTINOS KARETSAS

Karetsas is a young player in a hurry. He made his professional debut in Belgium's second tier at the age of just 15, playing for Genk's U–23 team. The left-footed playmaker caught the eye with a series of spectacular goals and was quickly promoted to Genk's senior side. Born in Belgium to Greek parents, Karetsas was subject to a tug-of-war between the two national federations before committing himself to Greece. His first outing for the *Ethniki* came in Mar 2025, and he made an immediate impact (*see below*). With talk increasing that Karetsas will move on to a major European club, it looks like his profile is only set to grow.

YOUNGEST GOAL SCORER IN THE UEFA NATIONS LEAGUE

On 23 Mar 2025, Karetsas (b. 19 Nov 2007) struck during Greece's 3–0 away win over Scotland aged 17 years 124 days. It was only his second international, having debuted in the first leg of the League A/B play-off. Karetsas scored on the same night as Spain's Lamine Yamal, with both players beating the previous record.

CLASS OF '27

AYYOUB BOUADDI

Given his classy and composed midfield play, it's hard to believe that Lille's Ayyoub Bouaddi (b. 2 Oct 2007) is still a teenager. He made his senior debut aged 16 years 3 days, lining up against Faroese side KÍ Klaksvík on 5 Oct 2023 to become the **youngest player in the UEFA Conference League**. Although this record has since been beaten (*see p.71*), Bouaddi's stock remains high. On his 17th birthday, he made an eye-catching debut in the UEFA Champions League as Lille beat Real Madrid 1–0. With a host of Europe's biggest clubs circling, he looks set for a career at the highest level.

Bouaddi is a high achiever both on and off the field. He won a national public-speaking contest for academy footballers at the age of 15, and is currently studying for a maths degree.

ASSIST ACE

On 5 Oct 2024, Bouaddi supplied his first Ligue 1 assist, teeing up Mitchel Bakker during Lille's 2–1 win over Toulouse. Aged 17 years 3 days, Bouaddi just missed out on the record for the **youngest player to make an assist in Ligue 1**. This is held by Eduardo Camavinga (AGO, b. 10 Nov 2002), who set up a goal for Rennes against Paris Saint-Germain aged 16 years 281 days on 18 Aug 2019.

LAMINE YAMAL

Already one of the biggest names in world football, Lamine Yamal has smashed a host of club and international records. A graduate of Barcelona's famous youth academy, La Masia, he made his first league appearance at the age of just 15. On 8 Oct 2023, Yamal (b. 13 Jul 2007) became the **youngest goal scorer in La Liga**, netting during a 2–2 draw with Granada aged 16 years 87 days. He had made his international debut the previous month, scoring for Spain during a 7–1 win over Georgia. At Euro 2024, Yamal broke records galore as he helped *La Roja* to the title (*see p.99*), scoring a memorable opening goal against France in the semi-finals.

YOUNGEST GOAL SCORER IN A UEFA CHAMPIONS LEAGUE SEMI-FINAL

Yamal was aged 17 years 291 days when he struck in Barcelona's 3–3 first-leg draw with Inter Milan on 30 Apr 2025. He beat Kylian Mbappé's record of 18 years 140 days, set in 2017. The seesawing semi-final ended in disappointment for Barça, however, as they lost 7–6 on aggregate after the second leg.

KOPA KING

The Kopa Trophy is awarded to the best player aged 21 or under in world football. It is organized by *France Football* magazine and decided by a jury made up of former Ballon d'Or winners. In 2025, Lamine Yamal became the first player to win the trophy for a second time, finishing ahead of Désiré Doué.

CLASS OF '27

CASEY PHAIR

In 2023, 16-year-old striker Casey Phair was catapulted from academy football to the FIFA Women's World Cup, where she made a record-breaking appearance for South Korea (*see below*). Phair was so young that she didn't even play for a professional club. Born in South Korea, she moved to the USA when she was a baby. She agreed terms with NWSL side Angel City in Jan 2024 and made her league debut against Gotham FC on 18 Apr 2025. A loan move to Swedish side Djurgårdens IF followed, as Phair continues her footballing education.

On 26 Oct 2023, Phair hit a hat-trick against Thailand in an Olympic qualifier – her first goals in senior football!

YOUNGEST PLAYER AT THE FIFA WOMEN'S WORLD CUP

Phair (b. 29 Jun 2007) was 16 years 26 days old when she appeared as a second-half substitute for South Korea against Colombia on 25 Jul 2023. The Korean-American phenom took the record from the late Ifeanyi Chiejine of Nigeria by just eight days. Phair featured in all three of South Korea's games at the World Cup, making her first start in their final group match against Germany.

CLASS OF '27

LILY YOHANNES

After moving to the Netherlands from the USA at the age of 10, Lily Yohannes caught the eye of Dutch giants Ajax while playing in a boys' team. She signed a professional contract at 15, and word of her precocious talent began to spread. On 15 Nov 2023, Yohannes (b. 12 Jun 2007) became the **youngest player to start a UEFA Women's Champions League group match**, lining up for Ajax against Paris Saint-Germain aged 16 years 156 days (*below*). She moved to women's superpower OL Lyonnes in Jul 2025, announcing her arrival with a debut goal against Marseille.

Yohannes's grandfather, Bokretsion Gebrehiwot, was an Ethiopian international who scored at the 1968 Africa Cup of Nations.

DECISION DAY

Yohannes was eligible to represent both the USA and the Netherlands at international level and faced a difficult decision between the two. She made her debut for the USA in a friendly against South Korea in Jun 2024 and scored within minutes of coming on. On 11 Nov 2024, Yohannes publicly committed to the USA, stating that "the US is my homeland, my birthplace".

CLASS OF '27

ESTÊVÃO WILLIAN

Electrifying winger Estêvão was just 10 years old when he signed a professional contract with Nike. At 16, he made his first-team debut for Palmeiras in Brazil's Série A, terrifying defences with his trickery and invention. He racked up 27 goals and 15 assists in 83 games, earning a move to Chelsea in Aug 2025 – having played his final game for Palmeiras against them at the FIFA Club World Cup, scoring in a 2–1 defeat. Estêvão soon became a fan favourite in West London, firing home an injury-time winner against Liverpool on 4 Oct 2025 to record his first goal for the club. He also became a fixture for Brazil, scoring five goals in 11 games.

YOUNGEST WINNER OF THE BOLA DE OURO

The Bola de Ouro ("Golden Ball") has been handed out annually to the best player in the Brazilian championship since 1973. Former winners include Neymar and Ronaldinho. On 9 Dec 2024, Estêvão (b. 24 Apr 2007) was awarded the Bola de Ouro at the age of 17 years 229 days. He was recognized for a breakout season for Palmeiras, when he scored 13 goals and made nine assists.

On 25 Nov 2025, Estêvão lined up against fellow teenage sensation Lamine Yamal as Chelsea took on Barcelona in the UEFA Champions League. And it was the Brazilian who stole the show, scoring a dazzling solo goal as Chelsea won 3–0.

CLASS OF '27

VICKY LÓPEZ

Spanish sensation Vicky López (b. 26 Jul 2006) is on the fast-track to superstardom. The Barcelona midfielder began her career at Madrid CFF, making her debut against Athletic Club on 5 Sep 2021 at the age of 15 years 41 days – making her the **youngest player in Liga F**. On her 16th birthday, it was announced that López had been signed by Barcelona. Schooled at its world-famous academy, La Masia, she has gone on to win three Liga F and two UEFA Champions League titles, and dazzled on the national stage with Spain at the 2025 UEFA Women's Euros.

In 2023, López became Barça's youngest scorer in *El Clásico*, aged 17 years 116 days. She would later lose the record to Lamine Yamal by just 11 days.

PRIZE POSSESSION

At the 2025 Ballon d'Or awards, López became the first-ever winner of the Women's Kopa Trophy, given to the best player aged under 21. She finished three points ahead of Real Madrid's Linda Caicedo in the voting. López scored 10 goals for Barcelona as they won the league, and played a key role for Spain at the Women's Euros.

CLASS OF '27

DÉSIRÉ DOUÉ

With his record-breaking exploits in the 2025 UEFA Champions League final, Désiré Doué catapulted himself into the top tier of world football talent. He burst into the Rennes first team at 17, his quicksilver midfield performances persuading Paris Saint-Germain to pay €50 m ($54.9 m) to sign him. In Doué's first season in Paris, he won the Young Player awards for both Ligue 1 and the UEFA Champions League as PSG marched to the treble. On 23 Mar 2025, he made his senior debut for France, having won an Olympic silver medal with the U-23 national team at the 2024 Games.

GOLDEN YEAR

Founded by Italian newspaper *Tuttosport* in 2003, the Golden Boy prize is awarded to the best men's player aged under 21 in a top-flight European league. Previous winners include Lionel Messi (2005), Kylian Mbappé (2017) and Lamine Yamal (2024). On 1 Dec 2025, Doué joined their ranks as he was recognized for his stellar season with PSG.

MOST GOAL INVOLVEMENTS IN A UEFA CHAMPIONS LEAGUE FINAL

Doué scored twice and set up Achraf Hakimi as Paris Saint-Germain routed Inter Milan 5–0 on 31 May 2025. This is the most goal involvements – three – by a player in the final since the competition was rebranded from the European Cup for the 1992/93 season.

CLASS OF '27

ARDA GÜLER

A left-footed midfield magician, Arda Güler's skills earned him the nickname the "Turkish Messi". He joined Fenerbahçe at the age of 13; at 17, he became the youngest-ever goal scorer for the Yellow Canaries. Güler's precocious displays attracted the attention of Europe's biggest clubs, and in 2023 he was snapped up by Real Madrid. A series of injuries disrupted his season, but he soon made up for lost time, scoring five times in five games. Güler has now firmly established himself as a first-team regular in Madrid.

On 14 Mar 2026, Güler scored a sensational goal against Elche from 68 m (223 ft) out. It was the first goal scored from a player's own half in La Liga for 15 years.

YOUNGEST GOAL SCORER ON DEBUT AT THE UEFA EUROPEAN CHAMPIONSHIPS

Güler (b. 25 Feb 2005) was 19 years 114 days old when he scored for Türkiye against Georgia on 18 Jun 2024. His arrowing shot from outside the box made Güler only the third teenager to strike on his Euros debut, after Hungary's Ferenc Bene in 1964 and Cristiano Ronaldo in 2004. Türkiye won the Group F encounter at Borussia Dortmund's Westfalenstadion 3–1.

FEATURE

PEERLESS PITCHES

No matter where they are, football lovers will find a way to play. Take a tour around some of the most unusual grounds on the planet, from the Arctic Circle to the Andes mountains – proving that, once and for all, football truly is THE global game...

KOH PANYEE, THAILAND
This island fishing settlement loved football so much that they built their own pitch on the water! The first surface was fashioned from wooden planks laid over floating fish cages. Upgrades include a 6-ft-high (1.8-m) net around the perimeter to stop the ball going into the water, but passing boats can still make the pitch wobble.

ALPENSIA SKI JUMPING STADIUM, SOUTH KOREA
In 2017, Korean outfit Gangwon FC played at a stadium with an unusual feature – two giant ski jumps behind one of the goals! Built for the 2018 Winter Olympics, the 11,000-capacity arena was adapted for football by laying a pitch over the landing area. Fans faced a daunting trek halfway up a mountain to reach the remote ground.

IGRALIŠTE BATARIJA, CROATIA
The home of Croatian side HNK Trogir is literally a fortress! Perched on an island in the historic town, the stadium is sandwiched between not one but two UNESCO World Heritage Sites – Kamerlengo Castle and St Mark's Tower. With three sides of the ground surrounded by water, Igralište Batarija has to be one of Europe's most picturesque grounds.

TASIILAQ STADION, GREENLAND

Despite the lack of grass in the Arctic Circle, football remains a popular sport in Greenland. The ground in Tasiilaq was built in 1960 and is home to local side ATA 1960. There's room for around 500 spectators but not much by way of seating – instead, you can settle down on the volcanic rocks and take in the panoramic view, which is dominated by the snowy peaks of Qimmeertaajaliip Qaqqartivaa.

HENNINGSVÆR STADION, LOFOTEN ISLANDS, NORWAY

This out-of-the-way settlement in the Norwegian Sea has found fame thanks to its football pitch. Created by levelling the island bedrock, Henningsvær Stadion is ringed by fish-drying racks and boasts a backdrop of stunning scenery. During the Arctic summer, locals can play at night without turning on the floodlights, thanks to the midnight sun.

ESTADIO HERNANDO SILES, LA PAZ, BOLIVIA

Situated at around 3,600 m (11,800 ft) in the Andes mountains, the Hernando Siles Stadium is one of the highest-altitude grounds on Earth. The air is so thin that players sometimes require oxygen after matches – Brazilian star Neymar claimed that conditions were "inhuman", following a tie against Bolivia in 2017.

CLASS OF '27

LINDA CAICEDO

An explosive and skilful attacker for both Colombia and Real Madrid, according to Linda Caicedo, "my style is one that's played on the streets". She started playing football at five and grew up as the only girl on her academy team. At 15, she was hit with a devastating blow when she was diagnosed with cancer. Caicedo underwent surgery and six months of chemotherapy, but was back at training just days after receiving the all-clear. Following a star-making turn for Colombia at the 2022 Copa América Femenina, she signed for Real Madrid in 2023.

YOUNGEST PLAYER IN THE FIFPRO WOMEN'S WORLD 11

The FIFPRO Women's World 11 is an annual award voted for by professional footballers to honour the best players in their positions. The team for 2024 was announced on 9 Dec and included Caicedo (b. 22 Feb 2005), who was then aged 19 years 291 days. She was recognized for her displays for Real Madrid and for Colombia at the 2024 Olympics (*above*).

PRIDE OF COLOMBIA

At the age of just 17, Caicedo was voted Player of the Tournament at the 2022 Copa América Femenina, scoring the winning goals against Ecuador and in the semi-final against Argentina. The following year, Caicedo once again grabbed the spotlight, this time at the FIFA Women's World Cup (*above*). She scored the Goal of the Tournament with a jinking run and finish against Germany as underdogs Colombia upset the odds to win 2–1.

CLASS OF '27

OLIVIA SMITH

On 17 Jul 2025, Canadian striker Olivia Smith made history when she became the **first £1-m transfer in women's football**, moving from WSL side Liverpool to Arsenal for £1 m ($1.3 m). Her fee exceeded the £880,000 ($1.1 m) paid by Chelsea to San Diego Wave for US defender Naomi Girma in Jan 2025. As the first £1-m player in the women's game, the 20-year-old Smith had a lot to live up to, but she has the game to back it up. Technically gifted, quick and strong, she is the epitome of the modern striker.

MADE IN CANADA

Smith was just 15 years old when she made her international debut against Brazil in 2019, becoming Canada's youngest-ever women's player. She scored her first senior goals against El Salvador and Paraguay at the 2024 CONCACAF W Gold Cup, earning her the Young Player Award.

LEAGUES APART

Despite her young age, Arsenal had seen enough in Smith's potential to break the bank for her. She first moved to Europe in 2023, signing for Portuguese side Sporting CP. Smith adapted seamlessly to her new league, racking up 22 goal involvements in 18 games. She then switched to England's WSL, joining Liverpool (*above*). Smith finished the season as club top scorer with seven league goals, and was voted PFA Young Player of the Year.

Smith's record for the **most expensive women's football transfer** lasted barely a month before it was beaten by Mexico's Lizbeth Ovalle, who moved from Tigres UANL to Orlando Pride for £1.1 m ($1.4 m) on 21 Aug 2025.

CLASS OF '27

MANAKA MATSUKUBO

The 2025 NWSL season was a breakout one for Manaka Matsukubo of the North Carolina Courage. The attacking midfielder had arrived at the club from Japanese side Mynavi Sendai in Jul 2023, initially on loan. Matsukubo gave immediate notice of her talent at the NWSL Challenge Cup, scoring against Racing Louisville FC and winning final MVP, despite being the youngest player in the competition. In 2025, Matsukubo went up another level, racking up 11 goals – the third-highest total in the league. She was named NWSL Midfielder of the Year.

YOUNGEST PLAYER TO SCORE A HAT-TRICK IN THE NWSL

Matsukubo (b. 28 Jul 2004) was 21 years 81 days old when she scored three goals against Bay FC on 17 Oct 2025. She struck twice in the opening eight minutes and added a third in the second half. Her treble propelled North Carolina Courage to a 4–1 win and earned Matsukubo the NWSL Player of the Week award.

CLASS OF '27

JUDE BELLINGHAM

All-action midfielder Jude Bellingham came through the ranks at Birmingham City before making an eye-catching move to Borussia Dortmund at the age of just 17. He spent three seasons in the Bundesliga before joining Real Madrid for €103 m (£88 m) in Jun 2023. In his first season in Spain, he scored 23 goals and won both La Liga and the UEFA Champions League. On 4 Nov 2025, Bellingham (b. 29 Jun 2003) became the **youngest player to make 50 appearances in the UEFA Champions League**, aged 22 years 128 days.

Bellingham had won 46 caps for England as of 20 Mar 2026. Perhaps his finest moment came against Slovakia at the 2024 UEFA Euros, when he scored an acrobatic overhead kick in injury time with England just moments from elimination. They went on to win the tie 2–1 after extra time.

GERMAN ADVENTURE

Bellingham set a number of records while playing for Borussia Dortmund. On 5 Oct 2022, he became the **youngest captain to score in the UEFA Champions League**, striking against Sevilla aged 19 years 98 days. Four months later, aged 19 years 235 days, Bellingham took the record for the **youngest player to win 50 Bundesliga matches** from Bayern Munich's Jamal Musiala.

CLASS OF '27

JAMAL MUSIALA

At the age of just 22, Jamal Musiala had already won five Bundesliga titles and the UEFA Champions League. He spent part of his childhood in the UK and played for the Chelsea academy before returning to Germany to join Bayern Munich. In 2020, he became the club's youngest-ever player and goal scorer, and although both records have since been beaten, Musiala has gone from strength to strength. Even a six-month spell on the sidelines following an injury at the 2025 FIFA Club World Cup couldn't stop the attacking midfielder's rise.

MOST GOALS IN A FIFA CLUB WORLD CUP MATCH

On 15 Jun 2025, Musiala came off the bench for Bayern to score a second-half hat-trick against Auckland City. The lopsided encounter ended in a 10–0 victory for the German side. Musiala became only the fifth player to score a hat-trick at the FIFA Club World Cup, following in the footsteps of Luis Suárez (URY), Cristiano Ronaldo (PRT), Gareth Bale (UK) and Hamdou Elhouni (LBY). Palestine's Wessam Abou Ali (b. DNK) added his own treble a week after Musiala.

HOME FAVOURITE

Musiala has played more than 40 times for Germany to date, having chosen to represent *Die Mannschaft* ("The Team") over England. On 11 Oct 2021, he scored against North Macedonia aged 18 years 227 days to become Germany's second-youngest scorer. At Euro 2024, Musiala shone on home soil, scoring three goals to earn himself a share of the Golden Boot.

CLASS OF '27

TRINITY RODMAN

Known for her lightning pace and relentless pressing, Trinity Rodman is a force of nature on the field. She was the youngest player to be drafted into the NWSL when the Washington Spirit selected her as a second-overall pick in Jan 2021. Rodman had a stellar debut season, winning the NWSL Rookie of the Year award and helping the Spirit claim their first-ever championship title. Her first USA call-up came the following year. Now established as one of the top talents in the NWSL, Rodman signed a blockbuster new deal with the Spirit in Jan 2026 with a reported value of more than $2 m (£1.4 m) a year.

YOUNGEST GOAL SCORER IN THE NWSL PLAYOFFS

Rodman (b. 20 May 2002) was 19 years 178 days old when she scored for the Washington Spirit in their championship semi-final tie against OL Reign on 14 Nov 2021. The Spirit won the game 2–1 and went on to defeat the Chicago Red Stars by the same score in the championship match, with Rodman once again in the starting line-up.

Rodman was a key member of the USA team who won gold at the 2024 Summer Olympics in Paris. She scored three times, and described her game-winning strike against Japan in the quarter-finals as the "best moment of my career".

Rodman took just 5 min to score her first senior goal, after coming off the bench against North Carolina Courage in the NWSL Challenge Cup on 10 Apr 2021.

CLASS OF '27

COLE PALMER

English midfielder Cole Palmer came through the ranks at Manchester City and was part of their treble-winning 2022/23 squad. Following a £40-m ($50-m) transfer to Chelsea, he racked up 22 goals and 11 assists in his first EPL season, earning the Premier League Young Player of the Season award. Nicknamed "Cold" for his ice-cool temperament, Palmer is a playmaker who loves the big stage. He has also made his mark on the international scene, scoring against Spain in the final of the 2024 UEFA European Championship.

FASTEST EPL PERFECT HAT-TRICK FROM KICK-OFF

On 15 Apr 2024, Palmer struck three times against Everton in the first 29 min, scoring one goal each with his right foot, left foot and head (*above*). He completed his perfect hat-trick with a beautifully judged lob over goalkeeper Jordan Pickford.

GOING FOR GOLD

At the 2025 FIFA Club World Cup, Palmer took centre stage as Chelsea sprang a surprise in the final, defeating European champions Paris Saint-Germain 3–0. Palmer stole the show with two goals and an assist for João Pedro – all before half-time. The Englishman finished the tournament with five goal involvements and was awarded the Golden Ball for best player.

CLASS OF '27

KLARA BÜHL

A winger equally comfortable on either foot, Klara Bühl is one of Europe's most dangerous attacking talents. She joined Bayern Munich from Freiburg in 2020 and won four league titles in five years. Bühl has already played 76 times for Germany, scoring 30 goals. At the UEFA Women's Euros in 2022, she was voted into the official Team of the Tournament, despite being ruled out of the semi-final and final owing to COVID-19. Bühl was also a mainstay of the German team that won a bronze medal at the 2024 Olympics in Paris.

ASSIST ACE

With her vision, passing ability and set-piece delivery, Bühl is a striker's dream. During Bayern's UEFA Women's Champions League tie with Arsenal on 12 Nov 2025, Bühl inspired a stunning second-half fightback, setting up three goals as Bayern came from 2–0 down to win 3–2.

LONGEST UNBEATEN STREAK IN THE FRAUEN-BUNDESLIGA

Bühl was a key member of the Bayern Munich side that went 44 league games without defeat between 30 Oct 2022 and 12 Oct 2024 – when they finally fell to a 2–0 defeat against VfL Wolfsburg. Munich claimed back-to-back league titles during their epic run, which included an entire season unbeaten in 2023/24.

CLASS OF '27

HANNAH HAMPTON

England's No.1 hit the headlines during the 2025 UEFA Women's Euros, saving two spot-kicks in successive penalty shootouts against Sweden and Spain as the Lionesses defended their trophy. Hampton was voted into UEFA's Team of the Tournament – then, on 22 Sep 2025, she became the first winner of the women's Yashin Trophy for goalkeeper of the year (*below*). It completed a remarkable journey for the Chelsea stopper, who was born with eye misalignment and was advised by doctors to avoid playing sport when she was younger.

YOUNGEST GOALKEEPER TO MAKE 100 WSL APPEARANCES

Hampton (UK, b. 16 Nov 2000) was 23 years 353 days old when she reached a century of league games, during Chelsea's 5–0 win over Everton on 3 Nov 2024. She made her WSL debut at 18, playing 50 games for Birmingham City and then 35 for Aston Villa. Hampton moved to Chelsea in Jul 2023, winning back-to-back championships in 2024 and 2025.

Hampton lived in Spain as a child and played as a striker for Villarreal's youth team. She didn't become a goalkeeper until she joined Stoke back in England.

ERLING HAALAND

With his strength, speed and ice-cool finishing, Erling Haaland is one of the deadliest strikers on the planet. He left his native Norway in 2019 for Red Bull Salzburg, where he scored 29 times in 27 games, including a hat-trick on his UEFA Champions League debut. More goals followed at Borussia Dortmund, where he finished as the Champions League top scorer in 2020/21. The following year, Haaland moved to Manchester City for €60 m (£51 m), and immediately began laying waste to EPL defences. Just how many goals will he go on to score – and how many records can he break?

Haaland set an age-category world record when he was just five, leaping 1.63 m (5 ft 4 in) in the standing long jump.

MOST GOALS IN AN EPL SEASON

Haaland enjoyed a dream debut season in England, scoring 36 times in 35 games for Manchester City in 2022/23. He hit four hat-tricks, including two in his first five league games. The previous EPL record of 34 goals, held jointly by Alan Shearer and Andy Cole, had been set when there were 42 games in a season rather than 38.

GOAL RUSH

At the U-20 World Cup in 2019, Haaland gave notice of his talent when he scored nine goals against Honduras. Despite winning 12–0, Norway failed to qualify for the knockout stages – but Haaland's haul was enough to earn him the Golden Boot. No player has scored more goals in a match at any FIFA 11-a-side tournament.

CLASS OF '27

VINÍCIUS JÚNIOR

A forward blessed with speed and outrageous dribbling skills, Vinícius Júnior is one of the most dazzling players in world football. His professional career began at Flamengo in his home country of Brazil – he made his debut at 16, and agreed to join Real Madrid after just 17 min of senior football. Moving to Spain in 2018, Vinícius soon wowed crowds with his ability. He made his first appearance for Brazil the following year: to date, Vinícius has played 45 times for the *Seleção*, scoring eight times. He captained his country in a friendly against Spain on 26 Mar 2024. Later that year, he was voted the Best FIFA Men's Player.

FINAL BOSS
The 2026 Supercopa de España final against Barcelona was Vinícius's 15th major final for Real Madrid. Incredibly, he had won 11 of them. Vinícius scored the only goal in the 2022 UEFA Champions League decider against Liverpool and struck again two years later (*above*), as Madrid beat Borussia Dortmund 2–0. Aged 23 years 325 days, he became the **youngest player to score in two UEFA Champions League finals**.

FASTEST UEFA CHAMPIONS LEAGUE GOAL BY A SUBSTITUTE
On 21 Oct 2020, Vinícius struck just 15 sec after coming off the bench in the 59th min for Real Madrid against Shakhtar Donetsk. Sadly, there were no fans present to witness this record-breaking goal, as the game was played under COVID-19 restrictions at the Alfredo Di Stéfano Stadium. The game ended in a shock 3–2 defeat for Real.

CLASS OF '27

BARBRA BANDA

Striker Barbra Banda has terrorized defences around the world. At club level, she played in Spain and China before joining the NWSL's Orlando Pride in 2024 for $740,000 (£581,655) – the second-highest fee ever in the women's game at that point. Banda scored eight goals in her first seven games and finished the regular season with 13, hitting another four in the playoffs as the Pride won the NWSL championship. Banda has also broken records playing for Zambia. At the 2023 FIFA Women's World Cup, she scored the 1,000th goal in the tournament's history as the Copper Queens beat Costa Rica 3–1.

MOST HAT-TRICKS IN OLYMPIC WOMEN'S FOOTBALL

Banda has hit three Olympic trebles for Zambia. She recorded hat-tricks in successive games for the Copper Queens at the delayed 2020 Tokyo Olympics, against the Netherlands and China, and added another against Australia in Paris three years later. Remarkably, Zambia didn't win any of these games, drawing 4–4 with China and losing 10–3 against the Netherlands and 6–5 to Australia.

Banda was named MVP of the 2024 NWSL Championship match after scoring the only goal of the game. Orlando Pride defeated Washington Spirit 1–0 to claim their first-ever NWSL title.

Football wasn't Banda's only sporting love growing up. She was also a professional boxer, who won all five of her bouts before deciding to concentrate on football.

JULIÁN ALVAREZ

Wherever Julián Alvarez goes, trophies follow. Versatile and hard-working, he is the ultimate team man who can play across the forward line. He made his debut for River Plate in 2018, winning the Copa Libertadores in his first season. On his 22nd birthday, it was announced that he would be moving to Manchester City. Alvarez spent two seasons in England, winning six major trophies. In 2024, Atlético Madrid signed him for a potential €95 m (£81 m). He has enjoyed arguably even greater success on the international stage, claiming two Copa América titles and the 2022 FIFA World Cup with Argentina.

MOST GOALS IN A COPA LIBERTADORES MATCH

On 25 May 2022, Alvarez struck six times as River Plate demolished Peruvian side Alianza Lima 8–1 at the Estadio Monumental in Buenos Aires, Argentina. The 22-year-old equalled the feat of Juan Carlos Sánchez (ARG), who scored six goals for Blooming against Deportivo Italia on 7 Apr 1985.

SEASON OF SILVERWARE

The 2022/23 season was one Alvarez will never forget. He was part of the Argentina team that lifted the FIFA World Cup in Qatar, scoring twice in the semi-final against Croatia. He then returned to Manchester City for the resumption of the European club season, going on to win the EPL, FA Cup and UEFA Champions League. Alvarez became the first player to win the World Cup and a European treble in the same season.

CLASS OF '27

KYLIAN MBAPPÉ

The oldest player on our Class of '27 list, Kylian Mbappé needs no introduction. A two-time FIFA World Cup finalist, he honed his skills at Clairefontaine, the French national football academy. Mbappé made his debut for Monaco in Dec 2015, aged 16, and won the Ligue 1 title the next year. A transfer to Paris Saint-Germain followed, where he won six more championships and became the club's all-time record scorer, with 256 goals. In Jun 2024, Mbappé earned his dream move to Real Madrid. He finished his debut season as La Liga's top scorer, netting 31 times in 34 games to earn the European Golden Shoe for the first time in his career.

YOUNGEST PLAYER TO SCORE 100 GOALS IN THE FRENCH TOP DIVISION

Mbappé (b. 20 Dec 1998) was 22 years 91 days old when he reached a century of Ligue 1 goals on 21 Mar 2021. A brace for Paris Saint-Germain against Lyon saw him better the mark set by Saint-Étienne's Hervé Revelli in 1969 by more than a year. Mbappé went on to score 191 Ligue 1 goals before moving to Real Madrid, including 16 for Monaco.

NATIONAL TREASURE

Mbappé earned his first cap for France in 2017, aged 18. The following year, he became only the second teenager, after Pelé, to score in a FIFA World Cup final. France beat Croatia 4–2 to lift the trophy (*above*). Four years later, Mbappé reached the final again, hitting a hat-trick against Argentina to equal Geoff Hurst's record for the **most goals in a FIFA World Cup final** (*see p.153*).

GAMERS UNITED

Football videogaming is big business, and the battles waged on the virtual pitch can be every bit as fierce as those in real life. Explore the titles that have proved a hit with fans, and meet the gamers who've shown the skill and dedication to make it to the top.

Most critically acclaimed football videogame

Pro Evolution Soccer 3 – also known as *World Soccer Winning Eleven 7 International* (Konami, 2003) – has a table-topping Metascore of 93. Described by one reviewer as the "most definitive soccer game ever released", this PlayStation 2 classic earned praise for its authentic gameplay.

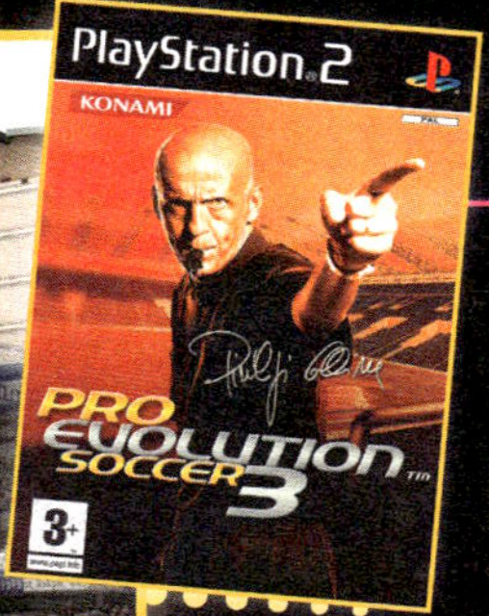

Longest game of *Football Manager*

Sepp Hedel (DEU, *above right*) spent 535 in-game years immersed in Sports Interactive's classic coaching sim between 2017 and 2025. He managed five clubs – FC United of Manchester, Bengaluru FC, Hereford FC, LA Galaxy and Tai Po FC – playing for more than 146 days in real life. Hedel reclaimed the record in 2025, having previously held it between 2019 and 2021.

Ecuadorian Adventure

Set in the Ecuadorian capital of Quito during the country's attempt to qualify for the 2002 FIFA World Cup, *Despelote* is the **most critically acclaimed football-themed adventure game**, with a Metascore of 89 for the PC. Players explore the streets as an eight-year-old with a football. The Ecuadorian national team did reach their first-ever World Cup in 2002 (*below*), chalking up an impressive 1–0 win over Croatia in the group stages.

Best-selling sports videogame franchise

More than 325 million units of the *EA Sports FC/FIFA* series have been sold since it kicked off in Dec 1993 with the release of *FIFA International Soccer*. Following *FIFA 23*, the franchise was reborn as *EA Sports FC*. The latest instalment boasted a playable roster of more than 20,000 male and female footballers, drawn from 750 clubs. At the ripe old age of 32, as of 2025, it is also the **longest-running football videogame series**.

FIFA 09 paired regular cover stars Ronaldinho and Wayne Rooney. The Manchester United star fronted seven consecutive main titles from *FIFA 06* to *FIFA 12* – the **most appearances on a *FIFA* videogame cover**.

"Nicolas99FC", aka Nicolas Villalba (ARG), is the **highest-earning *EA Sports FC/FIFA* player,** having won $851,431 (£635,438) from 54 tournaments as of 25 Mar 2026. Nicolas's most profitable year to date was 2022, when he won the eChampions League and finished second at the FIFA eWorld Cup, playing *FIFA 22*.

Highest-rated players on *EA Sports FC 26*

A quartet of players were awarded an overall rating of 91 for the latest instalment of EA's football sim. Mohamed Salah (EGY) and Kylian Mbappé (FRA, *above centre*) topped the men's rankings, while the Spain and Barcelona duo of Alexia Putellas and Aitana Bonmatí did likewise for the women. The lowest overall rating was 47, shared by 21 players.

Check out the ***Guinness World Records Gamer's Edition 2027*** for the very latest on gaming records.

NATIONAL LEAGUES

Since the foundation of the world's first league competition – the English Football League, in 1888 – the game has grown and grown. Currently a total of 211 nations and territories are part of FIFA, the world football federation. Take a tour around some of the world's biggest domestic championships, from Europe and Asia to North and South America.

CONTENTS

MOST CONSECUTIVE SEASONS IN THE ENGLISH TOP DIVISION

Arsenal celebrated their 100th successive top-flight season in style in 2025/26, winning the English Premier League for the first time since 2004. The Gunners were elected to the old First Division for the 1919/20 season, following the resumption of the Football League after World War I, and have remained in the top division ever since. They have been crowned champions of England on 14 occasions: 10 times in the First Division and four in the EPL era.

ENGLISH PREMIER LEAGUE

MOST WINS OF THE EPL SAVE OF THE MONTH AWARD
Jordan Pickford (UK) picked up his fourth EPL Save of the Month trophy in 2026, reward for his last-gasp acrobatic stop from a Sandro Tonali volley during Everton's 3–2 win at Newcastle United on 28 Feb (*below*). England No.1 Pickford had previously been honoured for saves against Liverpool (Sep 2022), Fulham (Jan 2024) and Manchester United (Nov 2025).

YOUNGEST EPL GOAL SCORER
Max Dowman (UK, b. 31 Dec 2009) was 16 years 73 days old when he scored a late breakaway goal for Arsenal against Everton on 14 Mar 2026. He beat the previous record – by Everton's James Vaughan, in 2005 – by 197 days. Dowman's record capped a stellar year for the teenage winger, who made his EPL debut at the age of 15.

MOST ASSISTS IN AN EPL SEASON
Bruno Fernandes (PRT, *below, second from left*) set up 21 goals for his Manchester United teammates in 2025/26. The Portuguese playmaker claimed the outright assist record on the final day of the season, when his corner was headed home by Patrick Dorgu. Fernandes's performances earned him the Premier League Player of the Season award.

MOST EPL APPEARANCES

On 21 Feb 2026, James Milner (UK) made EPL history by playing in his 654th game: Brighton's 2–0 win over Brentford. He made his debut, aged 16, for Leeds United in 2002, and played for six EPL clubs. Milner also holds the records for the **most EPL seasons played in** – 24 – and the **longest period between first and last EPL goals** – 22 years 248 days. He was presented with his certificates by GWR's Will Munford (*above*).

MOST EPL GOALS BY A FOREIGN PLAYER

From 2014 to 2026, Mohamed Salah (EGY) scored 193 English league goals: 191 for Liverpool and two for Chelsea. He surpassed Sergio Agüero's mark of 184 with a strike during Liverpool's title-clinching 5–1 win over Tottenham on 27 Apr 2025. Salah won two league titles and four Golden Boot awards while on Merseyside, also racking up the **most EPL goal involvements for one club** – 284.

Fulham's Raúl Jiménez (MEX) has taken the **most successful EPL penalties without missing**, converting his 14th spot-kick during a 3–1 victory over Burnley on 21 Mar 2026. The next best 100% record is held by Manchester City's Yaya Touré, with 11 flawless penalties.

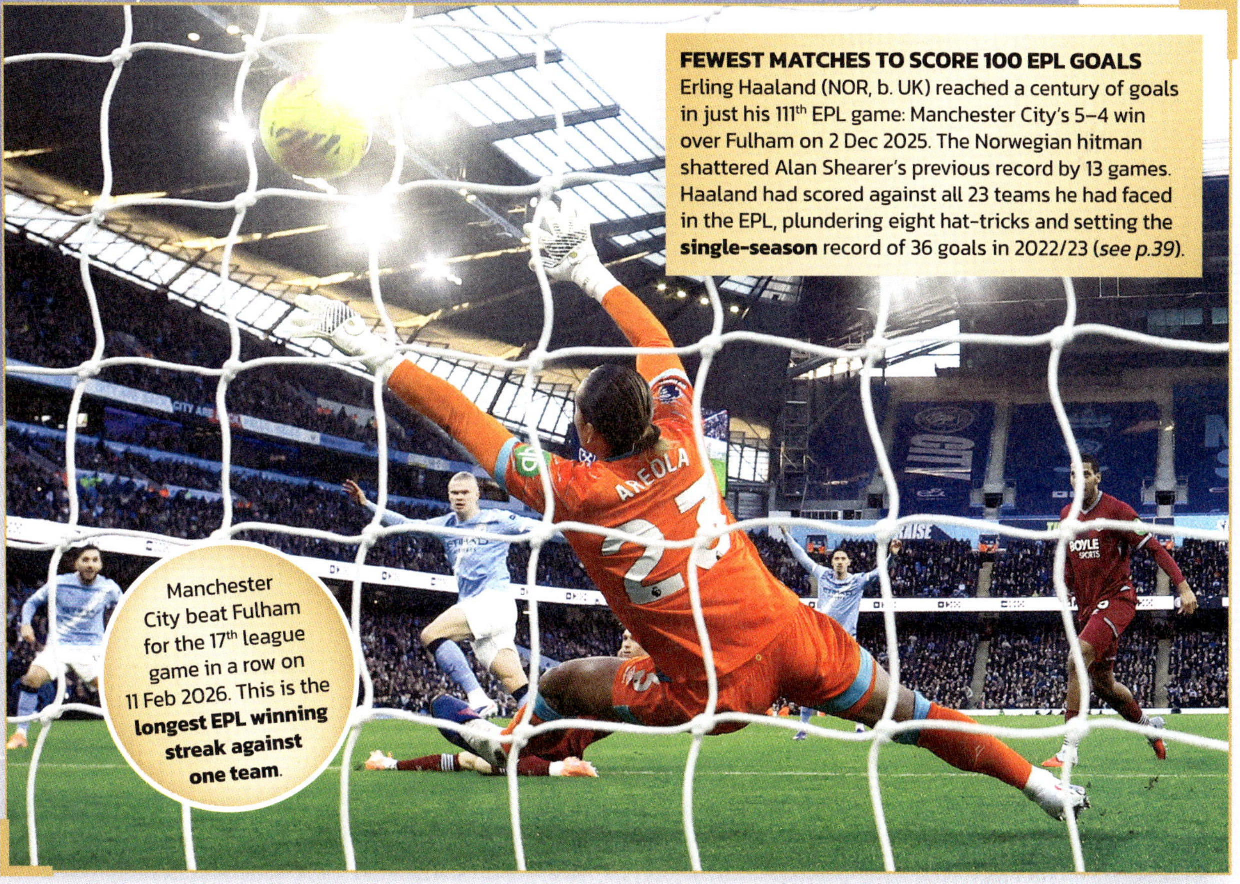

FEWEST MATCHES TO SCORE 100 EPL GOALS

Erling Haaland (NOR, b. UK) reached a century of goals in just his 111th EPL game: Manchester City's 5–4 win over Fulham on 2 Dec 2025. The Norwegian hitman shattered Alan Shearer's previous record by 13 games. Haaland had scored against all 23 teams he had faced in the EPL, plundering eight hat-tricks and setting the **single-season** record of 36 goals in 2022/23 (*see p.39*).

Manchester City beat Fulham for the 17th league game in a row on 11 Feb 2026. This is the **longest EPL winning streak against one team**.

LA LIGA

MOST VALUABLE FOOTBALL CLUB

Real Madrid were worth $9.5 bn (£7.1 bn; €8.2 bn) according to *Forbes*' 2026 Global Soccer Team Valuations. It was the fifth year in a row that *Los Blancos* had sat atop the financial rankings. They posted revenue of $1.27 bn (£946 m; €1.1 bn) for 2024/25, the highest figure ever recorded by a sports team. Real have amassed the **most wins of La Liga**, claiming 36 titles.

Real Madrid's Kylian Mbappé finished as La Liga's top scorer for the second year running in 2025/26, netting 25 times in 31 games. He reached 50 league goals in only his 53rd match, against Levante on 17 Jan 2026.

Griezmann's career total of 205 goals places him 11th on the list of La Liga's all-time top scorers.

MOST LA LIGA APPEARANCES BY A FOREIGN PLAYER

At the end of the 2025/26 season, Antoine Griezmann (FRA) departed for Major League Soccer having played 564 matches in La Liga. He spent 17 seasons in Spain, turning out for Atlético Madrid (349 games), Real Sociedad (141) and Barcelona (74). Griezmann surpassed Lionel Messi's record of 520 matches on 29 Mar 2025.

Basque side Athletic Club were one of the 10 teams to contest Spain's first season of the Primera División, staged in 1929, and have never been relegated. Together with Barcelona and Real Madrid, they share the record for the **most seasons in Spain's top division** – 95.

Ex-Spain international Santi Cazorla made an emotional return to La Liga in 2025/26 at the age of 40. He made 28 appearances for his hometown club, Real Oviedo, providing an assist against Real Sociedad.

YOUNGEST PLAYER TO MAKE 100 APPEARANCES IN LA LIGA

On 11 Apr 2026, Lamine Yamal (ESP, b. 13 Jul 2007) reached a century of games in the Spanish top flight at the age of 18 years 272 days. He celebrated with a goal and two assists as Barcelona beat Espanyol 4–1. Yamal – one of only five players to make his La Liga debut before the age of 16 – had scored 29 times, registering his first hat-trick against Villarreal on 28 Feb 2026.

MOST HOME WINS IN A LA LIGA SEASON (38 GAMES)

In 2025/26, Barcelona became the first La Liga team to win all 19 of their home games. They played their fixtures at three different grounds: Estadi Johan Cruyff, the Lluís Companys Olympic Stadium and the Camp Nou. Barça secured their 29th title with a 2–0 win over Real Madrid – the first time the championship had been decided in *El Clásico* since 1932.

BUNDESLIGA

LONGEST AWAY UNBEATEN STREAK IN THE BUNDESLIGA
Bayer Leverkusen went undefeated for 37 consecutive games on the road between 26 Aug 2023 and 18 Oct 2025, amassing 25 wins and 12 draws. Under coach Xabi Alonso, the team nicknamed "Neverlusen" went two complete seasons without losing an away game, also achieving the **first unbeaten Bundesliga season** in 2023/24. Their run finally ended with a 3–0 loss to Bayern Munich on 1 Nov 2025.

Eintracht Frankfurt hold the record for the **most different goal scorers in the Bundesliga**, with 299 players. Six players netted their first league goals for *Die Adler* ("The Eagles") in 2025/26, including top scorer Jonathan Burkardt (*immediate right, with Farès Chaïbi*).

MOST BUNDESLIGA RED CARDS
Dominik Kohr (DEU) received his marching orders for the ninth time during Mainz 05's 1–1 draw with TSG Hoffenheim on 21 Nov 2025. It was the third straight red card of his career. Kohr claimed the dubious honour outright, having previously shared it with former Germany international Jens Nowotny and Brazilian midfielder Luiz Gustavo.

Bayern's Michael Olise was voted the 2025/26 Bundesliga Player of the Season having scored 15 times and set up 19 goals, including three in one game. The dazzling winger fell just short of the **most assists in a Bundesliga season** – 21, by Thomas Müller (DEU) in 2019/20.

FEWEST GAMES TO ACHIEVE 100 GOAL INVOLVEMENTS IN THE BUNDESLIGA

On 21 Dec 2025, Harry Kane (UK) scored during Bayern Munich's 4–0 win over FC Heidenheim to reach a century of Bundesliga goal involvements in his 78th game. He scored 81 times and laid on 19 assists to beat Roy Makaay's record by 35 games. Sharpshooter Kane finished the 2025/26 season as the Bundesliga's top scorer for the third year in a row.

MOST BUNDESLIGA MATCHES WON

Manuel Neuer (DEU) emerged victorious from 375 of his 545 league games for Schalke 04 and Bayern Munich between 2006 and 2026. The goalkeeper claimed the record with his 362nd win on 18 Oct 2025. Neuer went on to win his 13th league championship in 2025/26, equalling his former teammate Thomas Müller's record for the **most Bundesliga titles**.

MOST GOALS IN A BUNDESLIGA SEASON

Bayern Munich blitzed the opposition in 2025/26, scoring 122 goals in 34 games – an average of 3.5 per match. Nineteen players made it on to the score sheet, topped by striker Harry Kane (*see above right*), who netted 36 times. Bayern's total was the second-highest in the history of Europe's top five leagues – behind only Serie A's Torino in 1947/48, who scored 125 goals in 40 matches.

Bayern have won the **most Bundesliga titles** – 34. They also won the championship in 1932, before the Bundesliga era began.

SERIE A

Turin giants Juventus have claimed the **most Italian top-flight titles** – 36, between 1905 and 2020 (*above*). Two further championships in 2005 and 2006 were stripped following the *Calciopoli* match-rigging scandal.

MOST SERIE A TITLES WON BY A MANAGER WITH DIFFERENT CLUBS

In May 2025, Antonio Conte (ITA) became the first coach to win Serie A with three different teams, having guided SSC Napoli to the title. He had previously claimed the *Scudetto* with Inter Milan (2021) and Juventus (2012–14) – with whom Conte claimed an additional five championships as a player. The master tactician has also succeeded outside of Italy, overseeing Chelsea's charge to the English Premier League title in 2016/17.

OLDEST PLAYER ON SERIE A DEBUT

On 23 Aug 2025, Luka Modrić (b. 9 Sep 1985) played his first Italian league game at the age of 39 years 348 days. The Ballon d'Or-winning Croatian midfielder turned out for AC Milan against Cremonese. On 13 Feb 2026, Modrić scored the winner in a 2–1 victory over Pisa to become the third-oldest scorer in Serie A history (*see below*).

Modrić followed in the footsteps of his childhood idol, Zvonimir Boban, who won four Serie A titles with AC Milan.

Oldest goal scorers in Serie A

PLAYER	TEAM	DATE	AGE*
Zlatan Ibrahimović (SWE)	AC Milan	18 Mar 2023	41:166
Alessandro Costacurta (ITA)	AC Milan	19 May 2007	41:25
Luka Modrić (HRV)	AC Milan	13 Feb 2026	40:157
Silvio Piola (ITA)	Novara	7 Feb 1954	40:131
Fabio Quagliarella (ITA)	Sampdoria	20 May 2023	40:109

(YY/DDD)

Nico Paz played a key role in Como's stellar 2025/26 season, scoring 12 times. The Spanish-born Argentine forward won the first-ever Serie A Rising Star of the Month award, for Aug 2025, and made it back-to-back wins the following month.

MOST SERIE A PLAYER OF THE MONTH AWARDS

Paulo Dybala (ARG) has received the league's monthly award – first handed out in Sep 2019 – on five occasions. He won his first with Juventus in Jul 2020 and received four more with AS Roma, including three in one season in 2023/24. Dybala is a five-time winner of Serie A.

Inter wing-back Federico Dimarco (ITA) produced the **most assists in a Serie A season** in 2025/26, setting up 18 goals with his deadly deliveries from the left-hand side. Dimarco surpassed the previous record of 16 with two assists against Torino on 26 Apr 2026.

MOST SEASONS PLAYED IN SERIE A

Inter Milan celebrated their 94th Italian top-flight campaign in 2025/26 in style, winning their 21st league title. They sealed the *Scudetto* with a 2–0 win over Parma on 3 May 2026, with goals from Marcus Thuram and Henrikh Mkhitaryan. The *Nerazzurri* ("Black and Blues") were Serie A's first-ever champions, in 1929/30, and remain the only side to have participated in every season since.

LIGUE 1

MOST SEASONS IN THE FRENCH TOP DIVISION

The 2025/26 Ligue 1 season was Olympique de Marseille's 76th in the top flight since the beginning of the professional era in 1932. This is six seasons more than their closest challengers, Saint-Étienne. Marseille are nine-time league champions and won the first-ever UEFA Champions League in 1992/93.

Brazil and Real Madrid star Endrick joined Olympique Lyonnais on a six-month loan in Dec 2025. He made an immediate impact, hitting a hat-trick away at Metz in his second league game. Aged 19 years 188 days, he became the fourth-youngest player to hit a Ligue 1 treble this century.

On 8 May 2026, Mezian Mesloub scored a vital winning goal against Nantes on his debut for Lens – just five seconds after coming off the bench! The Portuguese youth international was aged 16 years 181 days, making him the youngest player to score on Ligue 1 debut since Cyril Cassese for Toulon in 1989.

MOST ASSISTS IN LIGUE 1

Former French international Dimitri Payet (*right*) announced his retirement from football on 22 Mar 2026, ending an illustrious career in which he played 492 games in Ligue 1, scoring 103 goals and providing 106 assists. Payet played for four French sides in the top flight: Nantes, Saint-Étienne, Lille and Olympique de Marseille. Ligue 1 began collecting assist statistics in 2007/08.

The **most assists in a Ligue 1 match** is four, by Memphis Depay (NLD, *inset*) during Lyon's 5–0 win over Metz on 8 Apr 2018.

MOST WINS OF THE FRENCH TOP DIVISION
Paris Saint-Germain claimed their 14th top-flight league championship in 2025/26, seeing off challengers Lens 2–0 in the penultimate game of the season to seal the title. All but two of PSG's titles were won in the Ligue 1 era (2002–), in the aftermath of the club's takeover by Qatar Sports Investments in 2012.

PSG captain Marquinhos (BRA) has the **most wins of Ligue 1 by a player**, with an astonishing 11 titles in just 13 seasons at the club.

Fabián Ruiz (ESP) played 51 consecutive matches for PSG without losing a single one between 7 May 2023 and 25 Apr 2025 – the **longest unbeaten streak in Ligue 1 by a player**. Ruiz missed his side's defeats against Clermont, Nice and Toulouse, racking up 40 wins and 11 draws before PSG finally lost 3–1 to Nice.

LONGEST AWAY UNBEATEN STREAK IN LIGUE 1
Between 26 Feb 2023 and 3 May 2025, Paris Saint-Germain went on a run of 39 away games without defeat, winning 30 games and drawing nine. Their two-year streak finally came to an end with a 2–1 loss to Strasbourg. PSG surpassed AC Milan's 38 games in 1991–93 to record the longest unbeaten away run in Europe's top five leagues.

MAJOR LEAGUE SOCCER

HIGHEST MARGIN OF VICTORY IN AN MLS MATCH

On 13 Sep 2025, the Vancouver Whitecaps crushed the Philadelphia Union 7–0 to equal the biggest blowout in MLS history. Vancouver's new signing, Bundesliga legend Thomas Müller (*left*), became the first MLS player to score a hat-trick on his birthday. Five other teams – LA Galaxy, Chicago Fire, New York Red Bulls (twice), Atlanta United and Philadelphia Union – have also won a game by seven goals.

82,110

The **highest attendance at an MLS match**, for LA Galaxy against LAFC at the Rose Bowl in Pasadena on 4 Jul 2023.

MOST CONSECUTIVE GOALS BY TWO MLS TEAMMATES

Son Heung-min (KOR) and Denis Bouanga (GAB, b. FRA) scored all 18 of LAFC's goals between 23 Aug and 5 Oct 2025. The deadly duo's streak lasted for seven games and included three hat-tricks. Son had only made his LAFC debut on 9 Aug, following his reported $26.5-m (£20-m) transfer from Tottenham – a record fee for an incoming player to the MLS.

MOST GOAL INVOLVEMENTS IN AN MLS POSTSEASON

Lionel Messi (ARG) scored six goals and produced nine assists for Inter Miami in the 2025 MLS playoffs for a total of 15 goal involvements. In the MLS Cup final against the Vancouver Whitecaps on 6 Dec, Messi produced two moments of magic to assist his teammates as the Herons won 3–1 to claim their first MLS championship. He was named MLS Cup MVP.

Tadeo Allende (ARG) scored the **most goals in an MLS postseason** – nine – for Inter Miami in the 2025 playoffs. He surpassed Carlos Ruiz's previous record of eight with a 96th-min strike in the MLS Cup.

BRASILEIRO SÉRIE A

Flamengo, aka the Vultures, are Brazil's most popular club. Founded in 1911, they have never been relegated.

MOST TIMES TO WIN THE BRASILEIRO SÉRIE A AND COPA LIBERTADORES IN THE SAME SEASON

Flamengo claimed their second national-continental double in 2025, matching the feat of the legendary Santos team of 1962 and 1963. Under manager Filipe Luís, Flamengo finished three points clear of Palmeiras in the Brazilian top flight and defeated the same opponents 1–0 in the 2025 Copa Libertadores final. They won their first double in 2019, when they also reached the final of the FIFA Club World Cup.

MOST PROFESSIONAL FOOTBALL MATCHES PLAYED

No one in the history of the game has played more times than Brazilian keeper Fábio. On 20 Aug 2025, he lined up for his 1,391st match, overtaking England's Peter Shilton. Fábio played every minute of the 2025 Série A season for Fluminense. By the final league game on 7 Dec, he had increased his total to 1,417 matches. Fábio (b. 30 Sep 1980) also extended his record as the **oldest player in the Brasileiro Série A** to 45 years 68 days.

OLDEST GOAL SCORER IN THE BRASILEIRO SÉRIE A

Nenê (BRA, b. 19 Jul 1981) was 44 years 112 days old when he scored in Juventude's 3–1 win over Vasco da Gama on 8 Nov 2025. The veteran midfielder struck to record his third goal of the season. Nenê made his debut in 2002 and played in Spain, France and England before returning to Brazil. He surpassed goalkeeper Rogério Ceni as Série A's oldest scorer with a strike against Internacional in Aug 2024.

J1 LEAGUE

YOUNGEST J1 LEAGUE PLAYER

Maki Kitahara (JPN, b. 7 Jul 2009) was 15 years 237 days old when he made his Japanese league debut on 1 Mar 2025. The midfielder came on as a substitute during FC Tokyo's 2–0 loss to Kashima Antlers. He claimed the record from Takayuki Morimoto (JPN, b. 7 May 1988), who remains the **youngest J1 League goal scorer**, having netted aged 15 years 364 days on 5 May 2004.

In Apr 2025, GWR presented Yu Kobayashi (JPN) with his certificate for the **most goals by a substitute in the J1 League** – 29. The veteran striker has spent 16 seasons at Kawasaki Frontale. His 29th goal from the bench came during a 1–1 draw with Urawa Reds on 22 Nov 2024, which saw the game resume at half-time after the original match had been called off due to bad weather.

MOST WINS OF THE J1 LEAGUE

Kashima Antlers sealed their ninth J1 League title on a dramatic final day of the 2025 season, defeating Yokohama F. Marinos 2–1 to finish one point ahead of Kashiwa Reysol. It was Kashima's first championship since 2016, with previous wins coming in 1996, 1998, 2000–01 and 2007–09. They also broke the record for the **longest home unbeaten streak by a J1 League team**, going 27 games without a loss between 28 Oct 2023 and 6 Apr 2025.

Kashima translates as "Deer Island". Antlers fans can visit a deer enclosure at the local Shinto shrine before each game for good luck.

SAUDI PRO LEAGUE

MOST WINS OF THE SAUDI PRO LEAGUE

Al-Hilal have won eight titles since the Saudi top flight was rebranded as the Saudi Pro League in 2008/09. They claimed their most recent championship in 2023/24 in dominant fashion, winning 31 and drawing three of their 34 fixtures. The Riyadh-based side are Saudi Arabia's most decorated club, having won a total of 21 national championships since 1957.

The **youngest Saudi Pro League player** is Talal Haji (SAU, b. 16 Sep 2007). The teenage striker was 16 years 5 days old when he came on during Al-Ittihad's 2–1 win over Al-Fateh on 21 Sep 2023.

MOST ASSISTS IN THE SAUDI PRO LEAGUE

Al-Hilal's Salem Al-Dawsari (SAU) laid on 67 goals for his teammates between 2011 and 2026. He went past Yahya Al-Shehri's SPL record of 53 assists during Al-Hilal's 2–0 win over Al-Taawoun on 15 Mar 2025. Al-Dawsari set up a league-high 15 goals in 2024/25.

MOST GOALS IN A SAUDI PRO LEAGUE SEASON

Cristiano Ronaldo (PRT) struck 35 times for Al-Nassr in 2023/24, including four hat-tricks. The Portuguese superstar scored a brace against Al-Ittihad in the final game of the season to eclipse Abderrazak Hamdallah's total of 34 goals from 2018/19. It was the fourth national top-flight league in which Ronaldo had finished the season as top scorer.

NATIONAL WOMEN'S SOCCER LEAGUE

MOST REGULAR-SEASON APPEARANCES IN THE NWSL

Seattle Reign stalwart Lauren Barnes (USA, *far right, front*) retired at the end of the 2025 season having played 252 NWSL matches. The defender played all 13 seasons with the Reign, winning the NWSL Shield in 2014–15 and 2022. Barnes was the first player to achieve 150, 200 and 250 regular-season appearances.

On 29 Aug 2025, Kherrington "KK" Ream (USA, b. 8 Jul 2009) became the **youngest goal scorer in the NWSL**, aged 16 years 52 days. She came off the bench to score the second goal for the Utah Royals as they beat the Portland Thorns 2–1.

The **youngest NWSL player** is McKenna "Mak" Whitham (USA, b. 27 Jul 2010), aged 14 years 231 days. The US youth international appeared as a late substitute for Gotham FC during their 1–1 draw with Seattle Reign on 15 Mar 2025.

MOST WINS IN AN NWSL REGULAR SEASON

The Kansas City Current claimed the 2025 NWSL Shield in style, winning 21 of their 26 games. The Current's success was built on a miserly defence, which conceded just 13 goals, while striker Temwa Chawinga scored 15 times to win the Golden Boot for the second year in a row. In the playoffs, however, Kansas City went out in the quarter-finals, suffering a 2–1 loss to eventual champions Gotham FC.

WOMEN'S SUPER LEAGUE

Chelsea captain Millie Bright (*left, centre*) made the **most WSL appearances**, featuring in 216 games.

LONGEST UNBEATEN RUN IN THE WSL

Chelsea played 34 league games without defeat between 5 May 2024 and 7 Dec 2025, winning 28 and drawing six. Their run included the entirety of the 2024/25 season and the last three games of the season prior. The West London side surpassed their own WSL record of 33 games with a 1–1 draw against Liverpool on 16 Nov 2025. They also hold the record for the **most WSL titles** – eight, between 2015 and 2025 (*above*).

The **most WSL assists** is 54, by Beth Mead (UK) for Sunderland and Arsenal since 2015. Mead became the first player to reach 50 assists on the opening day of the 2025/26 season, with two against the London City Lionesses.

FASTEST WSL HAT-TRICK

It took Khadija "Bunny" Shaw (JAM) just 12 min 37 sec to score three goals during Manchester City's 5–2 victory over Tottenham Hotspur on 21 Mar 2026. The quick-fire treble extended Shaw's record for the **most WSL hat-tricks** to eight. Remarkably, half of these have come against Tottenham. Shaw has scored 83 times in the WSL to date. Her City teammate Vivianne Miedema (NLD) holds the record for the **most WSL goals**, with 97.

CELEBRITY SOCCER CLUB

They might have made their name outside of football, but our line-up of talented stars – arranged in a classic 4–4–2 formation – could give most sides a game. Several of them have played in the annual Soccer Aid match, showing off their skills for charity.

Maluma

Colombian rapper Maluma (aka Juan Luis Londoño Arias) is a regular on the US *Billboard* charts, but he could easily have stormed the football leagues instead. A left-footed midfielder, Maluma played for Atlético Nacional until he was 16, when he decided to concentrate on music. "Football was my life," he said.

Rowoon

An actor and former K-pop idol as a member of SF9, Rowoon (aka Kim Seok-woo) has also modelled for Tommy Hilfiger, his looks earning him the nickname "face genius". Rowoon is also a talented football player whose team once finished third in a national competition in South Korea.

Usain Bolt

Olympic sprint champion Usain Bolt (JAM) still holds the records for the **fastest 100 m** (9.58 sec) and the **fastest 200 m** (19.19 sec). Following the end of his athletics career, Bolt had trials at Borussia Dortmund and spent several weeks at Aussie outfit Central Coast Mariners, scoring twice in a friendly.

Chanelle Moon

K-pop star Chanelle Moon earned a whole new set of fans when clips of her playing football went viral across social media. A member of girl group FIFTY FIFTY, Moon has appeared alongside former Wales and Real Madrid star Gareth Bale for Korean football variety show *Next Legend*.

St Vincent

Guitar hero St Vincent (aka Annie Clark, USA) has won the **most Grammy awards for Best Alternative Music Album by a woman** – three. In 2014, Clark posted a YouTube video showcasing her skills doing a rainbow flick. She said the trick took three years to perfect during her high-school soccer days.

Diamond

Diamond – aka Livi Sheldon – has become famous battling contestants on the UK TV show *Gladiators*. But before she took up body-building, Sheldon played midfield and captained English side Worcester City Ladies. The 6-ft-tall (1.82-m) enforcer took part in Soccer Aid in both 2024 and 2025.

Bella Ramsey

The star of *The Last of Us* (HBO Max/ Sky Atlantic, *above left*), Ramsey is "obsessed" with football and showed off their skills at Soccer Aid 2025, lining up for the England XI. In 2024, Ramsey (UK, b. 25 Sep 2003) became the **youngest leading actress nominee at the BAFTA TV Awards**, aged 20 years 177 days.

Steve Nash

A two-time winner of the NBA's MVP award, Steve Nash lit up the basketball court with the Phoenix Suns, Dallas Mavericks and LA Lakers. But he could have just have easily turned pro as a soccer player after a promising youth career – just like his brother, Martin, who played 38 times for Canada.

Pavarotti received the **most curtain calls** – 165 – during an hour-long ovation in Berlin, Germany, on 24 Feb 1988.

Luciano Pavarotti

Italian tenor Pavarotti played in goal in his youth and had hopes of turning professional. Instead he became one of the most famous opera singers in history. His performance of the aria "Nessun Dorma" became the soundtrack to the 1990 FIFA World Cup in Italy.

Louis Tomlinson

As a member of pop group One Direction, Tomlinson became used to performing in front of screaming crowds. The boy band sold 70 million records and won the **most Teen Choice Awards** – 28. In 2013, Tomlinson signed for Doncaster Rovers as a non-contract player, turning out for their reserves.

Matt Smith

The 11th Doctor Who completed his first career regeneration as a teenager, turning to acting after a back injury ended his dreams of becoming a footballer. Smith played for youth teams at Nottingham Forest and Leicester City. In 2009, at the age of 26, he became the **youngest Doctor Who**.

CONTINENTAL CLUB TOURNAMENTS

The first meeting between two national league champions took place in 1895, when English title winners Sunderland defeated their Scottish counterparts Heart of Midlothian 5–3 in Edinburgh. Fast-forward 130 years, and now all six FIFA confederations have tournaments to decide their male and female continental club champions.

CONTENTS

MOST WINS OF THE UEFA CHAMPIONS LEAGUE/EUROPEAN CUP BY A COUNTRY

Spanish sides have been crowned champions of Europe on 20 occasions. The titles are shared between rivals Real Madrid (15) and Barcelona (five). Real claimed the first-ever European Cup in 1956 and the four titles that followed – the competition's **most consecutive wins**. Barcelona's first title arrived in 1992, the final year of the European Cup before it was rebranded as the UEFA Champions League. Barça have gone on to claim four titles since then (including 2011, *left*), while Real Madrid have won nine (including 2024, *below*).

Players from 54 different nations have won the Champions League or European Cup. Morocco and Ecuador joined the list in 2025, courtesy of PSG's Achraf Hakimi and Willian Pacho.

UEFA CHAMPIONS LEAGUE

MOST PENALTIES SCORED IN THE UEFA CHAMPIONS LEAGUE

On 21 Jan 2025, Robert Lewandowski (POL, *left*) put away a pair of spot-kicks during Barcelona's 5–4 win over Benfica to take his career total in the competition to 19. This equalled the mark set by Cristiano Ronaldo (PRT) for Manchester United, Real Madrid and Juventus between 2007 and 2020.

On 26 Nov 2025, David Luiz (BRA, b. 22 Apr 1987) headed home during Pafos's 2–2 draw with AS Monaco to record his first Champions League goal for eight years. At the age of 38 years 218 days, he became the second-oldest scorer in competition history. The **oldest goal scorer** is Pepe (PRT, b. BRA, 26 Feb 1983), aged 40 years 290 days, for FC Porto on 13 Dec 2023.

MOST UEFA CHAMPIONS LEAGUE MATCHES WON

Real Madrid (ESP) have won 208 games since the first season of the UEFA Champions League in 1992/93. They became the first club to log 200 victories on 16 Sep 2025, beating Marseille 2–1. The Spanish superpower have been crowned overall champions on 15 occasions, including six during the European Cup era (1955–1992). This is the **most wins of the UEFA Champions League**.

FEWEST MATCHES TO SCORE 50 GOALS IN THE UEFA CHAMPIONS LEAGUE

On 18 Sep 2025, Erling Haaland (NOR, b. UK) headed home against Napoli to reach a half-century of goals in just his 49th Champions League game. This was 13 matches quicker than the previous record, by Ruud van Nistelrooy. Haaland's goals came for Red Bull Salzburg (eight in six games), Borussia Dortmund (15 in 13) and Manchester City (27 in 31).

MOST FREE-KICK GOALS IN A UEFA CHAMPIONS LEAGUE KNOCKOUT MATCH

On 8 Apr 2025, Declan Rice (UK) fired home two spectacular free-kicks during Arsenal's 3–0 win over Real Madrid in their quarter-final first leg. He joined Rivaldo, Cristiano Ronaldo, Neymar and Hakim Ziyech as the only players to score two in a UEFA Champions League game – but the first beyond the group stages. Incredibly, Rice had never scored a free-kick in his previous 338 professional matches.

MOST CONSECUTIVE KNOCKOUT MATCHES WITH A GOAL INVOLVEMENT IN A UEFA CHAMPIONS LEAGUE SEASON

Khvicha Kvaratskhelia (GEO) provided a goal or an assist in seven knockout games in a row for PSG in 2025/26. The flying winger went on an unprecedented hot streak, totalling seven goals and three assists in this period, including braces against Chelsea and Bayern Munich. Kvaratskhelia was duly named UCL Player of the Season.

In 2025/26, PSG's Vitinha (PRT) completed the **most passes in a UEFA Champions League season** – 1,602, according to UEFA statistics. The midfield conductor beat the previous record of 1,299, by Barcelona legend Xavi in 2012/13.

MOST GOALS BY A TEAM IN A UEFA CHAMPIONS LEAGUE SEASON

Paris Saint-Germain (FRA) netted 45 times in 2025/26 as they successfully defended their title from the previous year. They matched Barcelona's record from 1999/2000 in the final against Arsenal, when Ousmane Dembélé converted a second-half spot-kick. PSG went on to lift the trophy after triumphing on penalties (*below*) following a 1–1 draw against the English champions.

UEFA EUROPA LEAGUE

Europe's second-tier club competition was first staged in its current form in 2009, replacing the UEFA Cup. In 2024/25, the Europa League adopted a new format, replacing the group stages with an expanded 36-team league phase – giving players even more opportunities to break records...

Unai Emery (ESP) has the **most wins of the Europa League by a manager** – 5. His latest triumph came on 20 May 2026, when his Aston Villa side beat Freiburg 3–0.

MOST APPEARANCES IN THE UEFA EUROPA LEAGUE

Dries Mertens (BEL) played 73 Europa League games, excluding qualifiers, from 2010 to 2025. He surpassed Rui Patrício's record of 69 during Galatasaray's 3–3 draw with Dynamo Kyiv on 21 Jan 2025. Mertens also featured for Utrecht, PSV Eindhoven and Napoli.

OLDEST GOAL SCORER IN A UEFA EUROPA LEAGUE KNOCKOUT MATCH

On 26 Feb 2026, Olivier Giroud (FRA, b. 30 Sep 1986) scored for Lille against Crvena Zvezda at the age of 39 years 149 days. The veteran marksman took just four minutes to find the net in Belgrade, Serbia. Lille won 2–0 to progress to the next round. (*For the Europa League's* ***youngest knockout scorer****, turn to p.16.*)

Bruno Fernandes (PRT) scored from the spot against Lyon in extra time. He has converted the **most Europa League penalties** – 12.

MOST GOALS IN A UEFA EUROPA LEAGUE MATCH

On 17 Apr 2025, Manchester United (UK) and Lyon (FRA) played out a nine-goal thriller in their quarter-final second leg at Old Trafford, with the English side winning 5–4 to progress 7–6 on aggregate. The score was 2–2 at the end of normal time – United fell 4–2 behind in extra time only to come roaring back, sealing victory with two goals in the final moments of the match.

CONTINENTAL CLUB TOURNAMENTS

UEFA CONFERENCE LEAGUE

Europe's third-tier club competition first took place in 2021/22, giving some of the continent's less-heralded teams the chance to shine. So far there has been a different winner each year – who will be the first side to triumph twice?

MOST GOALS SCORED IN THE UEFA CONFERENCE LEAGUE
Swedish striker Mikael Ishak netted 13 times for Lech Poznań between 2022 and 2026, excluding qualifying matches. He hit five during the 2022/23 Conference League and eight in 2025/26, claiming the outright goal record with a brace against Shakhtar Donetsk.

On 2 Oct 2025, AEK Larnaca's David Gerasimou (CYP, b. 2 Nov 2009) became the **youngest player in the UEFA Conference League**, coming on against AZ Alkmaar aged 15 years 334 days. The winger's play has earned comparisons with Ángel Di María.

Ismaïla Sarr (SEN) scored after just 21 sec of Crystal Palace's semi-final first leg against Shakhtar Donetsk on 30 Apr 2026. This is the **fastest goal in the UEFA Conference League**, beating the previous record of 32 sec by SK Rapid's Ferdy Druijf in 2022.

MOST MATCHES WON IN THE UEFA CONFERENCE LEAGUE
Fiorentina (ITA) have claimed victory in 29 games across four editions of the competition, excluding qualifying matches. *La Viola* reached two consecutive finals in 2023 and 2024, losing out to West Ham United and Olympiacos. Former Fiorentina striker Edin Džeko (BIH, b. 17 Mar 1986) is the **oldest goal scorer in the UEFA Conference League**, striking against SK Rapid at the age of 39 years 220 days on 23 Oct 2025.

Fiorentina's purple kit was supposedly born when their original red-and-white jerseys ran after being washed in the Arno River.

COPA LIBERTADORES

Held annually since 1960, the club championship of South America has been won by 27 different sides from seven countries. In recent years, the story has been one of Brazilian domination, with its teams lifting the trophy an incredible seven seasons in a row between 2019 and 2025.

MOST MATCHES WON AT THE COPA LIBERTADORES

On 2 Apr 2025, River Plate (ARG) became the first club to win 200 games in the Copa Libertadores, following a 1–0 victory over Peru's Universitario in Lima. They went on to extend their record to 202 before going out in the quarter-finals. River qualified for the tournament 41 times between 1966 and 2025, winning it in 1986, 1996, 2015 and 2018.

Alberto Spencer (ECU) scored the **most goals at the Copa Libertadores** – 54 – between 1960 and 1972. He hit 48 for Uruguay's Peñarol, with whom he won three titles, and six for Ecuador's Barcelona SC. Spencer's aerial ability earned him the nickname *Cabeza Mágica* ("Magic Head").

Independiente of Argentina were nicknamed *Rey de Copas* ("King of Cups") for their knockout successes.

Most wins of the Copa Libertadores

TEAM	COUNTRY	WINS	YEARS
Independiente	Argentina	7	1964–65, 1972–75, 1984
Boca Juniors	Argentina	6	1977–78, 2000–01, 2003, 2007
Peñarol	Uruguay	5	1960–61, 1966, 1982, 1987
Estudiantes	Argentina	4	1968–70, 2009
River Plate	Argentina	4	1986, 1996, 2015, 2018
Flamengo	Brazil	4	1981, 2019, 2022, 2025

YOUNGEST GOAL SCORER AT THE COPA LIBERTADORES

Ângelo Gabriel (BRA, b. 21 Dec 2004) was aged 16 years 106 days when he struck for Santos against San Lorenzo in Buenos Aires, Argentina, on 6 Apr 2021. His stoppage-time goal helped his side to a 3–1 away win in their qualifying-round tie.

By the end of the 2025 tournament, Club Nacional de Football (URY) had extended their record for the **most games at the Copa Libertadores** to 433. The 50-time champions of Uruguay have lifted the cup on three occasions: in 1971, 1980 and 1988.

FASTEST SENDING OFF IN A COPA LIBERTADORES FINAL

Botafogo midfielder Gregore (BRA, *right*) was shown a red card after just 1 min 4 sec of their showdown against Atlético Mineiro on 30 Nov 2024. He received his marching orders for a high boot on Fausto Vera, committed after just 29 sec. Botafogo overcame the early setback, however, to earn their first Copa Libertadores title with a 3–1 victory.

The **fastest sending off in a Copa Libertadores match** outright is 27 sec, by Alejandro Bernal (COL) for Atlético Nacional against Club Nacional de Football on 11 Mar 2014.

AFC CHAMPIONS LEAGUE ELITE

The search to find the club champions of the world's largest continent began in 1967, with the foundation of the Asian Champion Club Tournament. After a hiatus between 1971 and 1985, the competition returned – in 2002, it was renamed the AFC Champions League. The 2024/25 edition featured 24 teams, with league stages divided into East and West Regions.

MOST WINS OF THE AFC CHAMPIONS LEAGUE ELITE
Al Hilal of Saudi Arabia claimed their fourth continental title on 23 Nov 2021, following a 2–0 victory over South Korea's Pohang Steelers. Al Hilal's first two triumphs came in 1991 and 2000, when the tournament was called the Asian Club Championship. They also won in 2019, courtesy of a 3–0 aggregate defeat of Japan's Urawa Red Diamonds.

REPEAT CHAMPION
Roberto Firmino was named 2024/25 AFC Champions League Elite MVP after the former Liverpool frontman propelled Saudi side Al Ahli to the title with six goals and five assists. Together with teammates Riyad Mahrez and Édouard Mendy, Firmino became both an AFC and a UEFA Champions League winner.

Soufiane Rahimi (MAR) scored 13 times for Al Ain in 2023/24 to equal the record for the **most goals in an AFC Champions League Elite season.** He matched the feat of Muriqui (BRA) for Guangzhou Evergrande in 2013, Adriano (BRA) for FC Seoul in 2016, and Baghdad Bounedjah (DZA) for Al Sadd in 2018.

9
Seconds it took Sebastián Soria (QAT, b. URY) to score the **fastest AFC Champions League Elite goal**, for Lekhwiya vs Pakhtakor on 9 Apr 2013.

Montenegrin striker Dejan Damjanović racked up 42 goals for four clubs between 2009 and 2022.

Most goals scored in the AFC Champions League Elite

PLAYER	GOALS	CLUBS
Dejan Damjanović (MNE)	42	FC Seoul, Beijing Guoan, Suwon Samsung Bluewings, Kitchee
Lee Dong-gook (KOR)	37	Jeonbuk Hyundai Motors
Salem Al Dawsari (SAU)	35	Al Hilal
Nasser Al-Shamrani (SAU)	32	Al Shabab, Al Hilal, Al Ain, Al Ittihad
Elkeson (CHN, b. BRA)	30	Guangzhou Evergrande, Shanghai SIPG

The **biggest win in the AFC Champions League Elite** is 15–0, by Seongnam Ilhwa Chunma (KOR) against Persik Kediri on 11 May 2004, and Gamba Osaka (JPN) versus Da Nang on 22 Mar 2006.

MOST APPEARANCES IN THE AFC CHAMPIONS LEAGUE ELITE

Al Hilal winger Salem Al Dawsari (SAU) has played in 110 games since 2012. He became the first player to reach a century of appearances on 4 Feb 2025, celebrating with two goals in Al Hilal's 4–1 win over Persepolis. A two-time tournament winner, Al Dawsari finished the 2024/25 season as top scorer.

MOST WINS OF THE AFC CHAMPIONS LEAGUE ELITE BY A COUNTRY

South Korean teams have been crowned champions on 12 occasions since 1985/86. The titles are shared between six different clubs – the most successful are the Pohang Steelers, with three trophies. The most recent champions are Ulsan HD (*below*), who triumphed in 2020. South Korea's closest rival is Japan, with eight wins.

CONCACAF CHAMPIONS CUP

First held in 1962, this competition is contested by teams from North and Central America and the Caribbean. It has been dominated by Mexican sides, who have won 40 of the 60 editions held to date – with the 1978 title shared between three clubs.

MOST WINS OF THE CONCACAF CHAMPIONS CUP
On 1 Jun 2025, Cruz Azul (MEX) defeated Vancouver Whitecaps 5–0 in Mexico City to claim a record-equalling seventh title. It was *La Máquina's* first CONCACAF Champions Cup for 11 years. They equalled the feat of their crosstown rivals Club América (*left*), who lifted the trophy seven times between 1977 and 2016.

YOUNGEST PLAYER IN A CONCACAF CHAMPIONS CUP FINAL
Obed Vargas (MEX, b. USA, 5 Aug 2005) was 16 years 272 days old when he played in the second leg of Seattle Sounders' final against Pumas UNAM on 4 May 2022. The Alaskan-born midfielder helped Seattle to a 3–0 win, making it 5–2 on aggregate. They became the first US side to win the cup since 2000. The match at Lumen Field drew the **highest attendance for a CONCACAF Champions Cup match** – 68,741 spectators.

Striker Javier Orozco (MEX) scored the **most goals in the CONCACAF Champions Cup**, hitting 23 for Cruz Azul and one for Santos Laguna between 2008 and 2016. Nicknamed *Chuletita* ("Little pork chop"), Orozco finished as the competition's top scorer in 2008/09 (seven goals) and 2010/11 (a record 11).

Orozco scored four times in one Champions Cup game in 2010: Cruz Azul's thrilling 5–4 win over Real Salt Lake.

CAF CHAMPIONS LEAGUE

A tournament to decide the club champions of Africa was first held in 1964/65, won by Cameroon's Oryx Douala. The competition adopted its current name, the CAF Champions League, in 1997. Teams from North Africa have had the upper hand in recent years, providing the last nine champions. And 2025 saw a new name, Egypt's Pyramids, join the honour roll.

On 27 Sep 2019, the Mamelodi Sundowns (ZAF) humbled Côte d'Or of the Seychelles 11–1. This is the **highest margin of victory in a CAF Champions League match**, excluding preliminaries. The Sundowns are nicknamed The Brazilians on account of their yellow-and-blue kit.

Congolese striker Fiston Mayele finished as top scorer in the 2024/25 CAF Champions League with nine goals (including three in qualifying), as Egyptian side Pyramids secured their first-ever CAF Champions League title.

Al Ahly have achieved the **most wins of the CAF Champions League**, racking up 12 titles between 1982 and 2024.

LONGEST UNBEATEN RUN IN THE CAF CHAMPIONS LEAGUE

Al Ahly (EGY) went 27 games without defeat between 17 Mar 2023 and 3 Jan 2025, winning 19 and drawing eight across three seasons of the competition. The Red Devils rebounded from a 5–2 loss to the Mamelodi Sundowns to win the 2022/23 Champions League, and defended their title the following season without losing a match. The streak came to a surprise end with a 1–0 loss to Algeria's CR Belouizdad in the 2024/25 group stages.

UEFA WOMEN'S CHAMPIONS LEAGUE

SFK 2000 Sarajevo have achieved the **most seasons in the UEFA Women's Champions League**, competing in 23 of the 25 campaigns since the competition began in 2001. They have reached the last 32 four times.

YOUNGEST GOAL SCORER IN A UEFA WOMEN'S CHAMPIONS LEAGUE FINAL

Marta (BRA, b. 19 Feb 1986) was 18 years 79 days old when she scored for Sweden's Umeå against 1. FFC Frankfurt in the first leg of the 2004 UEFA Women's Cup final on 8 May. Umeå won the game 3–0 and the tie 8–0 on aggregate, with the young Brazilian superstar scoring three times.

The **most penalties scored in the UEFA Women's Champions League** is 11, by Arsenal's Kim Little. The Scotland midfielder is the Gunners' all-time leading scorer in the competition, having racked up 43 goals.

MOST MATCHES PLAYED IN THE UEFA WOMEN'S CHAMPIONS LEAGUE

OL Lyonnes' Wendie Renard (FRA) has made 135 appearances. The towering defender is one of only three players, with Alexandra Popp and ex-teammate Eugénie Le Sommer, to have logged a century of UWCL games. Renard has featured in 12 finals, winning eight of them – a record she shares with Le Sommer.

MOST GOALS IN THE UEFA WOMEN'S CHAMPIONS LEAGUE

Ada Hegerberg (NOR) is the league's all-time top scorer, with 69 goals between 2012 and 2026. The majority of these strikes – 65 – have come for OL Lyonnes, with an additional two goals each for Stabæk and 1. FFC Turbine Potsdam. Hegerberg overtook Anja Mittag's mark of 51 goals in only her 50th appearance in the competition.

MOST ASSISTS IN THE UEFA WOMEN'S CHAMPIONS LEAGUE

On 3 May 2026, Caroline Graham Hansen (NOR) laid on her 33rd goal in competition history, crossing for Salma Paralluelo during Barcelona's 4–2 semi-final second leg win over Bayern Munich to overtake Alexandra Popp's assist record. The elusive winger made her UWCL debut in 2011 and had previously played for Stabæk, Tyresö and VfL Wolfsburg.

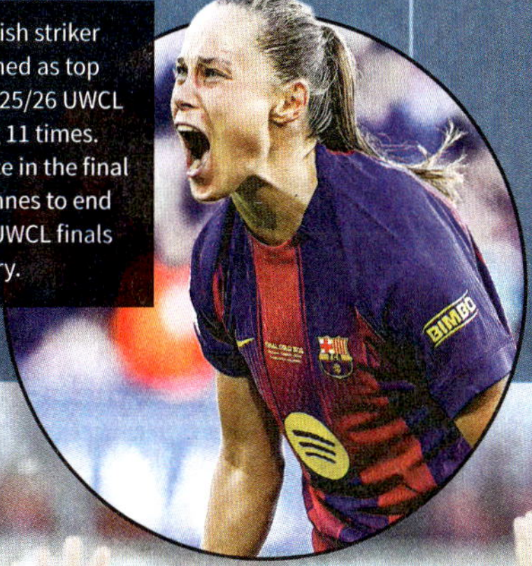

Barcelona's Polish striker Ewa Pajor finished as top scorer in the 2025/26 UWCL season, scoring 11 times. She netted twice in the final against OL Lyonnes to end her run of five UWCL finals without a victory.

MOST CONSECUTIVE UEFA WOMEN'S CHAMPIONS LEAGUE FINALS

Barcelona (ESP) reached their sixth successive final in 2026. They romped past OL Lyonnes 4–0 on 23 May in Oslo, Norway, to lift the trophy for the fourth time. It was the fourth occasion that the two heavyweights of European women's football had met in the final. Barça were formidable throughout the 2025/26 UWCL season, scoring 41 goals in 11 games – 15 more than any other team – and keeping the joint-most clean sheets – five.

CONTINENTAL CLUB TOURNAMENTS

COPA LIBERTADORES FEMENINA

The tournament to find the best side in South American women's club football was first held in 2009, with 17 editions to date. Brazilian teams have dominated the competition, winning 14 times, with additional triumphs for sides from Chile, Colombia and Paraguay.

MOST WINS OF THE COPA LIBERTADORES FEMENINA

On 18 Oct 2025, Corinthians (BRA) defeated Colombia's Deportivo Cali 5–3 on penalties in Banfield, Argentina, to claim their sixth title. Gabi Zanotti finished as top scorer for the second tournament in a row. Corinthians' previous triumphs came in 2017 – as a partnership with another Brazilian side, Audax – 2019, 2021 and 2023–24.

Corinthians recorded the **biggest win in a Copa Libertadores Femenina match** when they hammered Ecuador's El Nacional 16–0 on 5 Mar 2021. Three players scored hat-tricks.

The **youngest player at the Copa Libertadores Femenina** is Verónica Herrera (VEN, b. 14 Jan 2000), who was just 12 years 313 days old when she took to the pitch for Caracas's tie against Uruguay's Club Nacional on 22 Nov 2012. Caracas won the group-stage clash in Caruaru, Brazil, 2–0. Herrera currently plays her club football in Spain for SE AEM.

MOST GOALS AT A COPA LIBERTADORES FEMENINA TOURNAMENT

Striker Cristiane (BRA) scored 15 times at the first-ever championship in 2009. She bagged two five-goal hauls in the group stages as her side Santos laid waste to the opposition. Her overall tally might have been even higher, but she missed the final – which Santos won 9–0 – through suspension. Cristiane also finished top scorer at the 2012 tournament, netting seven times for São José.

CAF WOMEN'S CHAMPIONS LEAGUE

The 2025 tournament was only the fifth edition of the CAF Women's Champions League, but the competition is already making waves. Teams representing 40 countries from across the African continent battled it out in qualifying, with eight sides making the finals.

AS FAR's goalkeeper Khadija Er-Rmichi (MAR) has kept the **most clean sheets in the CAF Women's Champions League** – 15, across five editions. At the 2025 tournament she remained unbeaten until the final, conceding just one goal in five games.

MOST GOALS IN THE CAF WOMEN'S CHAMPIONS LEAGUE

Melinda Kgadiete (ZAF) scored seven times for Mamelodi Sundowns across four tournaments between 2021 and 2024. She found the net just 4 min into the Sundowns' first-ever Champions League game, against Vihiga Queens of Kenya. Kgadiete earned winner's medals in 2021 and 2023, and was also a member of the South Africa squad that lifted the Women's Africa Cup of Nations in 2022.

MOST WINS OF THE CAF WOMEN'S CHAMPIONS LEAGUE

On 21 Nov 2025, Morocco's AS FAR claimed their second Champions League title with a 2–1 victory over ASEC Mimosas of Côte d'Ivoire. Hanane Aït El Haj and Zineb Redouani scored a penalty in each half for AS FAR, who had previously won the tournament in 2022. They matched the feat of South Africa's Mamelodi Sundowns, two-time champions in 2021 and 2023.

ROUND-UP

Wherever you are in the world, there are increasing opportunities for your team to get a taste of continental glory. New tournaments and trophies, especially in women's football, are giving some new names a chance to step into the spotlight.

The top scorer of the 2025 Copa Sudamericana was 40-year-old Dayro Moreno, who netted 10 times in the competition for Colombian side Once Caldas.

MOST WINS OF THE COPA SUDAMERICANA

On 22 Nov 2025, Lanús (ARG) beat Brazil's Atlético Mineiro 5–4 on penalties to win South America's second-tier continental trophy for the second time. They joined two-time champions Boca Juniors, Independiente (both ARG), Athletico Paranaense (BRA), Independiente del Valle and LDU Quito (both ECU).

MOST CONSECUTIVE MATCHES UNBEATEN IN THE CONCACAF W CHAMPIONS CUP

Gotham FC (USA) didn't lose any of their first 10 games in this competition, designed to find the women's club champions of North and Central America and the Caribbean. They won the inaugural title on 24 May 2025, beating Mexico's Tigres UANL 1–0 with a goal from Esther González (*left*). The following season, Gotham added four more games to their unbeaten streak before finally losing in the semi-finals.

MOST WINS OF THE UEFA SUPER CUP

First held in 1973 (when it was called the Super Competition), the UEFA Super Cup pits the winners of UEFA's Champions and Europa Leagues against one another. Real Madrid lifted the trophy for a record sixth time in 2024, following a 2–0 victory over Italy's Atalanta. Their nearest challengers are AC Milan and Barcelona, both winners on five occasions.

The **fastest goal in the UEFA Super Cup** was scored after 50 sec by Diego Costa (ESP, b. BRA) in Atlético Madrid's 4–2 win over Real Madrid in 2018.

MOST WINS OF THE OFC MEN'S CHAMPIONS LEAGUE

On 12 Apr 2025, Auckland City (NZ) defeated Papua New Guinea's Hekari United 2–0 to become continental champions of Oceania for the 13th time. Their previous wins came in 2006, 2009, 2011–17 and 2022–24. Auckland City are so dominant that their closest rivals are the now-defunct Waitakere United, with two titles.

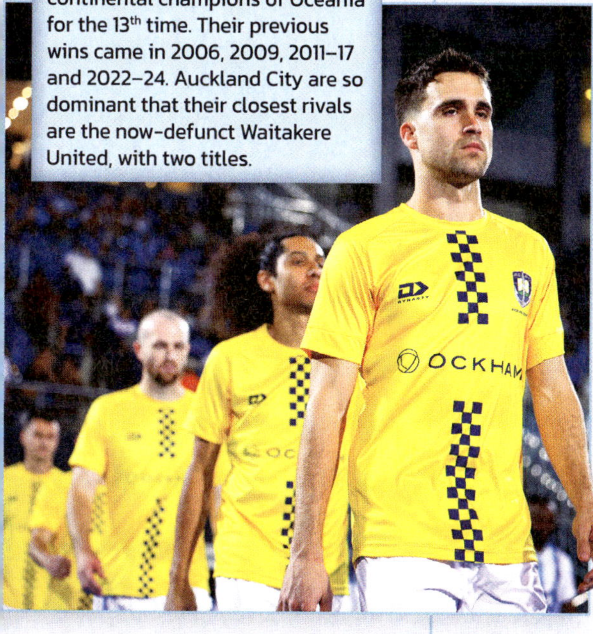

The first AFC Women's Champions League was decided on 24 May 2025. Following a 1–1 draw after extra time, China's Wuhan Jiangda defeated Melbourne City 5–4 on penalties. The new club champions of Asia pocketed $1.3 m (£960,000) for their efforts.

FEATURE

TRANSFER RECORD TIMELINE

Since the earliest days of association football, big-spending clubs have caused excitement and outrage by splashing out on players. Initially, it was largely English clubs who flexed their financial muscles, only for the Italian giants of Serie A to take over in the middle of the 20th century. In the 2000s, Real Madrid began assembling their team of *galácticos* – marquee players signed for eye-watering sums of money. But then, in 2017, a transfer took place that would dwarf all the others that had come before it...

ALF COMMON

Sunderland to Middlesbrough

£1,000

Common broke the world transfer record twice in under a year. In the summer of 1904, he signed for Sunderland for £520, before going for almost double that the following Feb. The first £1,000 transfer fee caused an outcry in the press, with one newspaper likening it to the slave trade! But Common's goals rescued Middlesbrough from relegation – he scored 58 times in 168 league games before moving to Woolwich Arsenal.

DAVID JACK

Bolton Wanderers to Arsenal

£10,890

Jack had enjoyed a successful nine-year spell at Bolton, winning the FA Cup twice in 1923 and 1926. His move to Arsenal made him the first £10,000 player. Under Arsenal's legendary manager Herbert Chapman, Jack won three English league championships. He became one of only three players in English football history, along with Jimmy Greaves and Alan Shearer, to score 100 top-flight goals for two clubs.

BERNABÉ FERREYRA

Tigre to River Plate

£23,000

Argentinian striker Ferreyra was famed for the power of his shooting – during a game for Vélez Sarsfield, he was said to have knocked an opposition goalkeeper unconscious after hitting him in the face with a shot! Ferreyra's transfer to River Plate for $50,000 (£23,000) saw the world transfer record broken outside the UK for the first time. He went on to score a staggering 187 goals in 185 matches.

1905

1928

1932

*eight transfers omitted

Sívori shares the record for the **most goals in a Serie A match**, hitting six against Inter Milan on 10 Jun 1961.

OMAR SÍVORI
River Plate to Juventus
£93,000

A quicksilver magician on the ball, Sívori was a dual international who played for both Argentina and Italy. He moved to Juventus at the age of 21, forming a fearsome forward line alongside Giampiero Boniperti and Wales's John Charles. Sívori spent a total of eight seasons in Turin, winning three league championships and earning himself the 1961 Ballon d'Or.

LUIS SUÁREZ
Barcelona to Inter Milan
£152,000

Suárez won the Ballon d'Or at Barcelona before becoming the first-ever Spanish player in Serie A. The elegant playmaker – nicknamed "The Architect" – became a key member of the legendary *Grande Inter* team under manager Helenio Herrera, winning three league titles and back-to-back European Cups. Suárez later managed Inter in three separate spells.

In 2024, Rodri became only the second Spanish-born men's player, after Luis Suárez, to win the Ballon d'Or.

ANGELO SORMANI
Mantova to Roma
£250,000

A Brazilian-born striker who went on to win seven caps for Italy, Sormani learned his trade at Santos, where he was a back-up for Pelé. In 1961, Sormani moved to Mantova in Italy, where he showed enough promise to invite a world-record bid from Roma. He spent just one season with the *Giallorossi* before moving on. Sormani would later find success at AC Milan (*above*), winning the league and European Cup.

1957

1961

1963

*six transfers omitted

FEATURE

TRANSFER RECORD TIMELINE

HARALD NIELSEN
Bologna to Inter Milan
£300,000

Danish centre-forward Nielsen had flourished in Serie A following his move to Bologna in 1961, twice finishing as the league's top scorer and winning the 1963/64 championship. However, his record-breaking move to Inter Milan proved ill-starred. Nielsen made just eight league appearances for the *Nerazzurri*, scoring twice, and retired three years later.

PIETRO ANASTASI
Varese to Juventus
£500,000

Anastasi (b. 7 Apr 1948) shot to fame playing for Italy at the 1968 Euros, where he became the **youngest goal scorer in a UEFA Euros final** aged 20 years 64 days. Transferring from Varese to Juventus for 660 million lire (£500,000), Anastasi became a huge fan favourite in Turin. He won three league titles and played in the 1973 European Cup final, a 1–0 loss against Ajax.

JOHAN CRUYFF
Ajax to Barcelona
£922,000

One of the most influential players in football history, Cruyff embodied the fluid Dutch philosophy of "Total Football". He led Ajax to three European Cups before moving to Barcelona for 6 million guilders (£922,000). In his first season at the Camp Nou, Cruyff brought Barça their first La Liga title in 14 years, and was on the scoresheet when the Catalans famously routed Real Madrid 5–0 away from home. He was duly awarded the Ballon d'Or for a third time.

Cruyff scored 33 goals in 48 games for the Netherlands. The Dutch never lost a match in which he scored.

1967

1968

1973

GIUSEPPE SAVOLDI

Bologna to Napoli

£1,200,000

A talented athlete and basketball player, on the football field striker Savoldi became famous for his aerial prowess and ice-cool penalty taking. He made his name at Bologna, winning the Coppa Italia twice and finishing the 1972/73 season as Serie A's top scorer. In 1975, Savoldi moved to Napoli for 2 billion lira, making him football's first million-pound player. He scored seven goals in his first seven games, but – despite winning a third Coppa Italia – Napoli were unable to mount a serious title challenge.

PAOLO ROSSI

Juventus to Vicenza

£1,750,000

Having converted from a winger to a striker, Rossi created history by finishing as Serie B and Serie A top scorer in consecutive seasons. At that point he was co-owned by Juventus and Vicenza, but a world-record fee made him the sole property of the latter. Rossi had an eventful club career that saw him loaned to Perugia and banned for two years. It was on the international stage where Rossi secured his legacy, winning the Golden Boot and Golden Ball at the 1982 FIFA World Cup as Italy lifted the trophy.

DIEGO MARADONA

Boca Juniors to Barcelona

£3,000,000

Barcelona had been tracking Maradona for years before they were finally able to sign him on the eve of the 1982 FIFA World Cup. Although illness and injury marred Maradona's brief stay at the Camp Nou, he still managed 38 goals in 58 appearances. His last game for Barça was the 1984 Copa del Rey final, during which he ended up at the centre of a mass brawl and was handed a three-month ban.

1975

1976

1982

TRANSFER RECORD TIMELINE

Napoli renamed its ground Stadio Diego Armando Maradona in the wake of his death in 2020.

DIEGO MARADONA

Barcelona to Napoli

£5,000,000

Having once again broken the world transfer record, Maradona firmly put his Catalan disappointment behind him. He transformed Napoli's fortunes almost single-handedly, steering them from the lower reaches of Serie A to their first-ever league championship in 1986/87. Maradona was the league's top scorer in 1987/88, won the UEFA Cup the following season and claimed a second Serie A title in 1990.

RUUD GULLIT

PSV Eindhoven to AC Milan

£6,000,000

Although often deployed behind the striker, Gullit could play almost any position. He scored 22 league goals for PSV in 1986/87, despite playing at centre-back for much of the season. After moving to AC Milan, Gullit picked up the 1987 Ballon d'Or before winning Serie A in his first season in Italy. Together with Marco van Basten and Frank Rijkaard, he was one of a trio of Dutch superstars at Milan, claiming two more league titles and two European Cups.

ROBERTO BAGGIO

Fiorentina to Juventus

£8,000,000

An elegant and sublimely talented attacker, "The Divine Ponytail" was so beloved by Fiorentina fans that news of his transfer to Juve caused riots in Florence. Baggio made it clear that he had been reluctant to move and refused to take a penalty against his old club the next season. He guided Juve to the UEFA Cup final in 1993, scoring twice in the first leg against Borussia Dortmund. The Ballon d'Or followed later that year.

Roberto Baggio is the only Italian player to score at three FIFA World Cups – 1990, 1994 and 1998.

1984

1987

1990

JEAN-PIERRE PAPIN

Marseille to AC Milan

£10,000,000

Striker Jean-Pierre Papin was Ligue 1's top scorer for five consecutive seasons, becoming famous for his spectacular volleys. He won four French championships and was awarded the 1991 Ballon d'Or. But Papin found it harder to establish himself at AC Milan and spent just two seasons at the San Siro, scoring 18 goals in 40 league games before moving to Bayern Munich.

GIANLUCA VIALLI

Sampdoria to Juventus

£12,000,000

One half of a deadly forward partnership with Roberto Mancini at Sampdoria – the pair were nicknamed the "Goal Twins" – Gianluca Vialli's goals spurred Sampdoria to their first-ever Serie A title in 1991. After a slow start to his Juve career, Vialli blossomed under manager Marcello Lippi. In four seasons in Turin, Vialli won another league title, the UEFA Cup and the 1995/96 Champions League, overcoming defending champions Ajax in the final.

GIANLUIGI LENTINI

Torino to AC Milan

£13,000,000

A riotously talented wideman, Lentini caught the eye with his displays for his hometown club, Torino, as they reached the 1992 UEFA Cup final. Following his move to AC Milan, Lentini won Serie A in his first season. In Aug 1993, however, he was involved in a high-speed car crash and was placed in an induced coma for two days. His career never truly recovered, and although he stayed at Milan until 1996, Lentini became an increasingly peripheral figure.

1992

1992

1992

TRANSFER RECORD TIMELINE

ALAN SHEARER

Blackburn Rovers to Newcastle United *£15,000,000*

Hot off the back of a superb Euro 1996 tournament, where he claimed the Golden Boot, Shearer moved to Newcastle for a world-record fee – despite reported interest from both Real Madrid and Manchester United. The hometown hero scored a hatful of goals on Tyneside, but was unable to bring the club the silverware they craved. Shearer did set a number of individual records, however, including the **most EPL goals** – 260.

RONALDO

Barcelona to Inter Milan

£19,500,000

Following a dazzling season for Barcelona, where he scored 47 goals in 49 games, Ronaldo caused dismay at the Camp Nou by moving to Inter Milan. In his first season, Ronaldo (b. 18 Sep 1976) became the **youngest winner of the Ballon d'Or**, aged 21 years 96 days, and his goals helped Inter lift the UEFA Cup in 1998. Although a series of serious knee injuries stopped Ronaldo in his prime, he would move to Real Madrid and win the 2002 World Cup with Brazil.

DENÍLSON

São Paulo to Real Betis

£21,500,000

One of the more eye-catching transfers on our list, tricky midfielder Denílson moved to La Liga from Brazil's São Paulo. He played nearly 200 times for Betis, including one season in the Spanish second division. Although Denílson's club career never really caught fire – featuring spells in Saudi Arabia, Greece and Vietnam – he played 61 times for Brazil, picking up a World Cup winner's medal in 2002.

1996

1997

1998

Vieri grew up in Australia and was a talented cricketer, his sporting idol the batter Allan Border.

CHRISTIAN VIERI

Lazio to Inter Milan

£32,000,000

A powerful forward with an eye for goal, Vieri played for a total of 13 clubs in a nomadic career. Inter were the only club where he spent more than one consecutive season. Over the course of six years in Milan, Vieri racked up 123 goals in 190 appearances. He won the Coppa Italia in 2005 and was Serie A's top scorer in 2002/03. Vieri played 49 times for Italy, scoring 23 goals.

1999

HERNÁN CRESPO

Parma to Lazio

£35,500,000

Argentina striker Crespo had made his name at Parma, winning the Coppa Italia and the UEFA Cup in 1998/99. His world-record move to Lazio saw two players move the other way in part-exchange. Crespo soon showed his value, finishing his first season in Rome as Serie A's top scorer with 26 goals. However, Lazio's financial issues meant that he moved on to Inter Milan after just two seasons.

Crespo scored in the UEFA Champions League for five clubs: Parma, Lazio, Inter Milan, Chelsea and AC Milan.

2000

When Figo returned to the Camp Nou in Nov 2002, a pig's head was thrown at him as he took a corner!

LUÍS FIGO

Barcelona to Real Madrid

£37,000,000

Barça fans were outraged when their idol Figo moved to arch-rivals Real Madrid. The winger won La Liga in his first season with Madrid and followed up with the 2001/02 Champions League. Figo's performances earned him the 2000 Ballon d'Or and the 2001 FIFA World Player of the Year award.

2000

FEATURE

TRANSFER RECORD TIMELINE

ZINEDINE ZIDANE

Juventus to Real Madrid

£46,500,000

A giant of the *galácticos* era, "Zizou" had already won the FIFA World Cup and the Ballon d'Or before joining Madrid in 2001. The following year, he struck a remarkable volley in the Champions League final against Bayer Leverkusen as Real prevailed 2–1. Zidane was renowned for his vision and close control – "he plays as if he had silk gloves on each foot," declared Madrid legend Alfredo Di Stéfano.

KAKÁ

AC Milan to Real Madrid

£56,000,000

Kaká's performances for Brazil and AC Milan had earned him the reputation as one of the world's best players. In 2007, he won the Ballon d'Or ahead of Ronaldo and Messi. But Kaká's time in Madrid was disrupted by injuries and the Brazilian playmaker made just 120 appearances for Real, scoring 29 times.

CRISTIANO RONALDO

Manchester United to Real Madrid *£80,000,000*

Real Madrid might have had to break the transfer record to secure his services, but "CR7" proved he was worth every penny. Ronaldo scored an astonishing 450 goals in 438 games, becoming the all-time top scorer for the Spanish giants. Two league titles and four UEFA Champions League trophies followed. Ronaldo received the Ballon d'Or four times while at Real, in 2013–14 and 2016–17.

2001

2009

2009

Pogba shares the record for the **most assists in an EPL game**, supplying four against Leeds on 14 Aug 2021.

GARETH BALE
Tottenham Hotspur to Real Madrid £85,000,000

Welsh wing wizard Bale had lit up the EPL with his dazzling performances for Tottenham, earning a big-money move to Real. Though his time in Madrid wasn't without controversy, Bale won three La Liga and five UEFA Champions League titles. His 106 goals for the club included spectacular efforts such as his solo run against Barcelona in the 2014 Copa del Rey final, and a bicycle kick against Liverpool in the 2018 Champions League final.

PAUL POGBA
Juventus to Manchester United £89,000,000

French midfielder Pogba returned to Manchester having spent three years there as a youth player. Despite enjoying great success in Serie A, where he guided Juve to four league titles, Pogba's second spell at United never hit the same heights. He went back to Turin in 2022.

NEYMAR
Barcelona to Paris Saint-Germain £198,000,000

Neymar's €222-m transfer sent shockwaves through football. Part of the fabled "MSN" attacking trio at Barça with Lionel Messi and Luis Suárez, Neymar's move signalled the intent of PSG's Qatari owners. The Brazilian superstar won Ligue 1 five times, but success in the Champions League eluded him. But the world's all-time transfer record had been shattered – possibly for ever...

2013 2016 2017

FEATURE

AMAZING AWAY DAYS

Long-distance away games offer fans the opportunity to prove their dedication to the cause. But even a diehard ultra might think twice before embarking on these time-zone-hopping journeys – across countries, continents and even the world...

SPORTING CP VS KAIRAT ALMATY

On 18 Sep 2025, Kazakhstan's Kairat Almaty embarked on the **greatest distance for a UEFA Champions League match**, flying 6,911 km (4,294 mi) to play Sporting CP at the Estádio José Alvalade in Lisbon, Portugal. Although Kairat were making their debut in the competition, the two sides had actually played three times before, in UEFA futsal competitions. But the Kairat fans who made the journey this time had little to cheer about, as their side went down to a 4–1 defeat.

Italian giants AC Milan and Inter Milan faced off in the 2002/03 UEFA Champions League semi-final with an official distance of 0 km between them. Despite playing both legs at the same stadium, the San Siro, AC Milan went through on "away" goals!

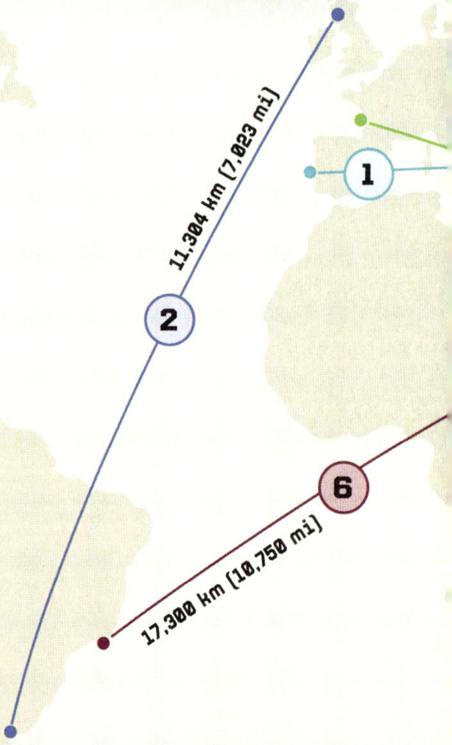

BRAZIL VS ZAMBIA

On 15 Oct 2013, Brazil lined up for an international friendly against 2012 AFCON champions Zambia... in Beijing, China. The nominal "home" side took to the field some 17,300 km (10,750 mi) from Rio de Janeiro. Oscar and Dedé struck for the South Americans as they ran out 2–0 winners. The globe-trotting *Seleção* went on to play friendlies in the USA and Canada before the year was out.

RACING AVELLANEDA VS CELTIC

In 1967, Celtic travelled 11,304 km (7,023 mi) to Argentina to take on Racing Avellaneda in the Intercontinental Cup – a competition that pitted the European champions against the winners of the Copa Libertadores. A total of 106 intrepid fans took a 29-hr flight from Scotland via the Cape Verde Islands. Celtic were 1–0 up from the first leg in Glasgow but went down to a 2–1 defeat at El Cilindro stadium. With no away goals rule, a deciding match was played three days later in Montevideo, Uruguay. Racing won 1–0.

FC LUCH-ENERGIYA VLADIVOSTOK VS FC KUBAN KRASNODAR

Vladivostok's presence in the Russian Premier League in 2006–08 caused travel headaches for other clubs, as it was situated in the far east of the country by the Sea of Japan. No club was farther away than Krasnodar (*fans pictured*) in southern Russia. The league ties between the two sides in 2007 involved the **greatest distance for a top-flight football league match** – a marathon 9,689 km (6,020 mi).

3 9,689 km (6,020 mi)

6,911 km (4,294 mi)

4 17,142 km (10,651 mi)

5 5,225 km (3,246 mi)

AS MAGENTA VS TRÉLISSAC FC

In Nov 2014, fourth-tier French outfit Trélissac FC undertook the **greatest distance for a football match** – an epic 17,142-km (10,651-mi) journey to New Caledonia, a French overseas territory in the South Pacific Ocean, to face off against AS Magenta in the Coupe de France. After a 27-hr flight via Japan, the globe-trotting Trélissac won the tie at Stade Numa-Daly Magenta 3–0 to progress to the next round.

PERTH GLORY VS WELLINGTON PHOENIX

A-League Men's "Distance Derby" sees New Zealand side Wellington Phoenix take on Perth Glory of Western Australia, with an each-way journey of around 5,225 km (3,246 mi). In 2015, the two teams began contesting the Long Distance Derby Cup, with the winner determined by head-to-head results across each season.

Perhaps the most remote football team on Earth plays on Tristan da Cunha. A handful of fixtures have been held on the South Atlantic island, despite the fact that it is 2,400 km (1,490 mi) from the nearest inhabited settlement.

CONTINENTAL INTERNATIONAL TOURNAMENTS

All six FIFA confederations have men's and women's continental championships, turning up the heat on local rivalries. South America led the way, holding the first men's Copa América back in 1916. It took 40 years before another continental competition followed, and almost 20 more before the first for women was staged (*see right*). But now they are some of the game's biggest and most fiercely contested tournaments.

CONTENTS

LONGEST-RUNNING INTERNATIONAL WOMEN'S FOOTBALL TOURNAMENT

The 2026 AFC Women's Asian Cup was the 21st edition in tournament history, and took place 51 years after the first in 1975. The 2026 final, staged at Sydney's Stadium Australia on 21 Mar, drew the **highest attendance at an AFC Women's Asian Cup match**. A crowd of 74,397 people saw Japan defeat Australia 1–0, thanks to a superb strike from Maika Hamano. It was Japan's third Asian Cup triumph in four tournaments – all of them secured with a 1–0 win over Australia in the final.

UEFA EUROPEAN CHAMPIONSHIP

The second-most-watched football tournament on the planet, behind the FIFA World Cup, the UEFA Euros have been staged 17 times since 1960. The first edition had just four teams – now more than 50 nations enter qualifying, in the hope of becoming one of the 24 finalists with a shot at European glory.

Martin Ødegaard (NOR, b. 17 Dec 1998) is the **youngest player in a UEFA Euros qualifier.** The precocious teenager came on as a substitute for Norway against Bulgaria aged 15 years 300 days on 13 Oct 2014.

YOUNGEST CAPTAIN AT THE UEFA EUROS

Hungary's Dominik Szoboszlai (b. 25 Oct 2000) led out his national side against Switzerland on 15 Jun 2024 at the age of 23 years 234 days. He laid on an assist for Barnabás Varga, but couldn't prevent Hungary sliding to a 3–1 defeat. Szoboszlai – who was handed the captaincy in Nov 2022 – was one of a number of youthful leaders at Euro 2024, including a pair of 25-year-olds: Italy's Gianluigi Donnarumma and France's Kylian Mbappé.

OLDEST GOAL SCORER AT THE UEFA EUROS

On 24 Jun 2024, Croatia captain Luka Modrić (*left*, b. 9 Sep 1985) netted during a 1–1 draw against Italy at the age of 38 years 289 days. He struck only seconds after having a penalty saved. Modrić became only the third player – alongside Portugal's Pepe and Cristiano Ronaldo – to play in five Euros tournaments. He has made more than 200 appearances for Croatia.

MOST GOALS AT THE UEFA EUROS

Cristiano Ronaldo (PRT) scored 14 times for Portugal across six tournaments between 2004 and 2024. His first-ever international goal came on his Euros debut, against Greece on 12 Jun 2004. Hungary were his most frequent victims, conceding four in two games. Ronaldo has also played the **most UEFA Euros games**, appearing in 30 matches.

YOUNGEST WINNER OF THE UEFA EUROS

Lamine Yamal (ESP, b. 13 Jul 2007) became a continental champion the day after his 17th birthday, following Spain's 2–1 win over England in the final of Euro 2024. The victory set the seal on a fairytale tournament for the talented teen, who had become the Euros' **youngest player** (16 years 338 days) against Croatia in the group stages, and the **youngest goal scorer** (16 years 362 days) against France in the semi-finals.

FACT

Radoslav Látal is the only player to be sent off twice at the Euros. The Czech Republic midfielder received his marching orders against Portugal in 1996 and the Netherlands four years later.

Most wins of the UEFA Euros

TEAM	WINS	YEARS
Spain	4	1964, 2008, 2012, 2024
Germany*	3	1972, 1980, 1996
France	2	1984, 2000
Italy	2	1968, 2020
Soviet Union	1	1960
Czechoslovakia	1	1976
Netherlands	1	1988
Denmark	1	1992
Greece	1	2004
Portugal	1	2016

**as West Germany in 1972 and 1980*

Spain became continental champions for a record fourth time at Euro 2024, defeating England 2–1 in the final at Berlin's Olympiastadion. They also racked up the **most goals by a team at a UEFA Euros tournament** – 15.

UEFA NATIONS LEAGUE

Introduced in 2018, the UEFA Nations League provides European sides with a competitive alternative to international friendlies. The tournament is arranged into four ranked leagues – A, B, C, D – with teams promoted and relegated depending on their season's results. There have been three winners to date: Portugal (2019 and 2025), France (2021) and Spain (2023).

Estonia's Patrik Kristal (b. 12 Nov 2007) is the **youngest player in the UEFA Nations League.** He was aged 16 years 301 days when he made his debut against Sweden on 8 Sep 2024, becoming his country's youngest-ever player.

BIGGEST WIN IN THE UEFA NATIONS LEAGUE

On 16 Nov 2024, Germany dismantled Bosnia 7–0 in a League A tie in Freiburg. Jamal Musiala opened the floodgates soon after kick-off (*above*), with further goals from Tim Kleindienst, Florian Wirtz (two each), Kai Havertz and Leroy Sané. Germany went on to reach the semis of the 2024/25 finals tournament.

MOST GOALS IN A UEFA NATIONS LEAGUE TOURNAMENT

Viktor Gyökeres scored nine times in six games for Sweden in League C of the 2024/25 UEFA Nations League. His tally included four against Azerbaijan on 19 Nov 2024 – this equalled the record for the **most goals in a UEFA Nations League match**, set by Armenia's Yura Movsisyan against Gibraltar on 16 Nov 2018. Gyökeres finished the 2024/25 campaign one goal ahead of Cristiano Ronaldo, who scored eight times for Portugal in League A and the finals.

MOST WINS OF THE UEFA NATIONS LEAGUE

On 8 Jun 2025, Portugal defeated local rivals Spain 5–3 on penalties to claim their second Nations League title. The action-packed game had finished 2–2 after extra time, with Nuno Mendes and Cristiano Ronaldo scoring for Portugal. Their first Nations League triumph came in 2018/19, when they dispatched the Netherlands 1–0 in the final.

Ronaldo (PRT, b. 5 Feb 1985) became the **oldest winner of the UEFA Nations League**, aged 40 years 123 days, when he lifted the trophy in Munich's Allianz Arena on 8 Jun 2025 (*see above*).

MOST UEFA NATIONS LEAGUE GOALS

Norway striker Erling Haaland (b. UK) struck 19 times between 2020 and 2024. His first international goal came in a Nations League B tie against Austria on 4 Sep 2020. Haaland is the only player to date to register two hat-tricks in the competition, versus Romania and Kazakhstan.

Most UEFA Nations League goals

PLAYER	TEAM	GOALS
Erling Haaland	Norway	19
Cristiano Ronaldo	Portugal	15
Aleksandar Mitrović	Serbia	15
Romelu Lukaku	Belgium	10
Vedat Muriqi	Kosovo	10
Viktor Gyökeres	Sweden	10

COPA AMÉRICA

The **longest-running continental football tournament** takes place in South America and was first held in 1916. The inaugural competition was contested by four teams – Argentina, Brazil, Chile and Uruguay – who have gone on to win 42 of the 48 tournaments to date.

MOST WINS OF THE COPA AMÉRICA

Argentina are 16-time champions of South America. They claimed their first title at the 1921 Copa América, and recorded the **most consecutive wins** of the tournament – three – between 1945 and 1947. Argentina endured a 32-year drought before claiming back-to-back wins in 1991 and 1993. They moved one clear of Uruguay's record of 15 titles in 2024, beating Colombia 1–0 in the final.

Venezuela and Ecuador are the only members of the CONMEBOL confederation who are yet to win the Copa América.

MOST MATCHES PLAYED AT THE COPA AMÉRICA

Lionel Messi (ARG) made 39 appearances across seven tournaments from 2007 to 2024. He lost three finals – in 2007, 2015 and 2016 – and even retired from international duty after missing a spot-kick in the 2016 shootout. Redemption came in 2021, when Argentina beat Brazil 1–0 in the final. In 2024, Messi lifted the trophy again (*above*).

Ecuador wonderkid Kendry Páez was just 17 years 53 days old when he converted a penalty against Jamaica in 2024 (*right*). The **youngest goal scorer at the Copa América** is Colombia's Johnnier Montaño (b. 14 Jan 1983), who struck against Argentina on 4 Jul 1999 at the age of 16 years 171 days.

Peru's all-time record scorer, Paolo Guerrero, played in his sixth Copa América in 2024 at the age of 40.

On 13 Jul 2024, Luis Suárez (URY, b. 24 Jan 1987) became the **oldest goal scorer at the Copa América**, aged 37 years 171 days. *El Pistolero* ("The Gunman") came off the bench to net a stoppage-time equalizer against Canada in the third place playoff.

Most goals scored at the Copa América

PLAYER	TEAM	GOALS
Norberto Méndez	Argentina	17
Zizinho	Brazil	17
Teodoro Fernández	Peru	15
Severino Varela	Uruguay	15
Paolo Guerrero (*above*)	Peru	14
Lionel Messi	Argentina	14
Eduardo Vargas	Chile	14

MOST ASSISTS IN A COPA AMÉRICA TOURNAMENT

James Rodríguez (COL) set up six goals for his Colombian teammates in 2024 – the highest total since the statistic was first monitored in 2011. He claimed the outright record in the semi-final against Uruguay, when his corner was nodded home by Jefferson Lerma. Rodríguez was named Best Player of the Tournament for his efforts. He has played more than 120 times for Colombia, winning the Golden Boot at the 2014 FIFA World Cup.

AFRICA CUP OF NATIONS

A total of 15 countries have been crowned champions of Africa since the first AFCON tournament was held in 1957. Back then, only three teams participated – Sudan, Egypt and Ethiopia. The 2025 tournament saw 24 sides battle it out, and the competition was fiercer than ever...

Mozambique legend Domingues (b. 13 Nov 1983) became the **oldest outfield player at the AFCON** at the 2025 tournament. The midfielder was aged 42 years 53 days when he captained the Mambas in their first-ever AFCON knockout game, a 4–0 defeat to Nigeria in the Round of 16 on 5 Jan 2026.

In 2023, Côte d'Ivoire pulled off one of the unlikeliest triumphs in AFCON history. After stumbling in the group stages, they sacked their head coach. Under interim boss Emerse Faé, Côte d'Ivoire roared back in the knockout stages and beat Nigeria 2–1 in the final.

MOST AFCON MATCHES PLAYED
Cameroon's Rigobert Song (*right*) and Ghana's André Ayew (*left*) both appeared in 36 AFCON games. Tough-tackling Song was a two-time winner in 2000 and 2002, when he was named Player of the Tournament. Ayew was joint top scorer in 2015, when Ghana finished as runners-up. The duo also share the record for the **most AFCON tournaments played** – eight – together with Ahmed Hassan (EGY) and Youssef Msakni (TUN).

MOST AFCON TOURNAMENT APPEARANCES BY A TEAM

Egypt have played in 27 editions of the AFCON. They first participated in 1957; two years later, they returned as the United Arab Republic, a sovereign union with Syria. The Pharaohs have racked up the **most AFCON wins**, triumphing on seven occasions, most recently in 2010.

The **most consecutive AFCON tournaments played by a team** is 17, by Tunisia between 1994 and 2025.

MOST AFCON GOALS

Samuel Eto'o scored 18 times for Cameroon between 2000 and 2010. He won the tournament twice and finished as top scorer in back-to-back tournaments in 2006 and 2008. Eto'o – a four-time winner of the African Player of the Year award – struck against 10 different sides. Angola were his favourite victims, conceding three times.

MOST CONSECUTIVE AFCON MATCHES SCORED IN

Brahim Díaz (MAR, b. ESP) struck in five games in a row for Morocco at the 2025 AFCON tournament. He scored in all three of Morocco's Group A games – against Comoros, Mali and Zambia – and followed up with the winner against Tanzania in the Round of 16. A further goal during Morocco's 2–0 win over Cameroon in the quarter-finals extended Díaz's record to five.

Despite finishing the 2025 AFCON with the Golden Boot award, Díaz's tournament ended in tears when he missed a penalty in the final.

AFC ASIAN CUP

First staged in 1956, the AFC Asian Cup is the second-oldest continental championship after the Copa América. The first tournament featured only four sides – Hong Kong, South Korea, Israel and South Vietnam. By 2019, the competition had expanded to 24 teams. It has been won by nine different countries, including Kuwait, South Korea and Australia.

FASTEST GOAL IN AN AFC ASIAN CUP MATCH

Just 14 sec were on the clock when Ali Mabkhout (UAE) scored against Bahrain on 15 Jan 2015, latching on to a through ball from Omar Abdulrahman before rounding the keeper. The UAE won the game in Canberra, Australia, 2–1. Mabkhout's total of 85 goals in 113 matches for his country puts him in the all-time top 10 men's international scorers.

The 2023 Asian Cup saw hosts Qatar claim their second title in a row. A growing force on the continent, the Maroons won five of their six games and saw off Jordan 3–1 in the final.

Tajikistan became the latest side to make their AFC Asian Cup debut at the 2023 edition, held in 2024. The newcomers qualified from their group and defeated the UAE on penalties to reach the quarters, where they were edged out 1–0 by Jordan.

MOST AFC ASIAN CUP TOURNAMENT APPEARANCES

Ignatiy Nesterov (UZB) played in five Asian Cups between 2004 and 2019. The goalkeeper claimed the outright record on 9 Jan 2019, when he took to the field against Oman in Sharjah, UAE. Nesterov's best tournament with the White Wolves came in 2011, when Uzbekistan reached the semi-finals.

MOST WINS OF THE AFC ASIAN CUP

Japan are four-time champions of Asia. The Samurai Blue came from nowhere to lift their first-ever international trophy in 1992, inspired by tournament MVP Kazuyoshi Miura. They won back-to-back titles in 2000 and 2004, defeating hosts China 3–1 in the 2004 final in front of a hostile crowd. At the 2011 tournament in Qatar, Japan saw off Australia 1–0 in extra time to claim their fourth Asian Cup victory.

MOST MATCHES PLAYED AT THE AFC ASIAN CUP

Japanese midfielder Yasuhito Endō featured in 21 games across four tournaments between 2004 and 2015. He won the competition twice, in 2004 and 2011, although he missed the first final after receiving a controversial red card in the semis.

Iran's Ali Daei scored the **most AFC Asian Cup goals**, netting 14 times at the 1996, 2000 and 2004 tournaments. Daei scored a total of 108 goals for Iran, giving him the record for the **most men's international goals** between 2003 and 2021.

Most matches won at the AFC Asian Cup

TEAM	TOURNAMENTS	GAMES PLAYED	GAMES WON
Iran	15	74	45
South Korea	15	73	38
Japan	10	53	33
Saudi Arabia	11	52	23
China	13	59	23

CONCACAF GOLD CUP

The Gold Cup is the most prestigious competition for national teams in the CONCACAF region: North and Central America and the Caribbean. It was first held in 1991, replacing the CONCACAF Championship. Over the course of 18 editions, just three teams have lifted the trophy – and the 2025 final saw a pair of old rivals do battle once more...

PLAYER PROFILE

Landon Donovan

Four-time winner Landon Donovan (USA) is the most successful player in Gold Cup history. He played in six tournaments between 2002 and 2013, setting records for the **most matches played** (34) and the **most goals** (18). Donovan finished as joint top-scorer three times – in 2003, 2005 and 2013 – and was awarded the Golden Ball in 2013.

Panama's Ismael Díaz is one of only two players, together with the USA's Jesús Ferreira, to score two Gold Cup hat-tricks. Against Qatar in 2023, Díaz produced the **fastest CONCACAF Gold Cup hat-trick**, scoring three times in nine second-half minutes. He hit another treble against Jamaica in 2025, with the goals all coming in the first half this time.

Most matches won at the CONCACAF Gold Cup

TEAM	TOURNAMENTS	GAMES WON
USA (*above*)	18	73
Mexico	18	67
Costa Rica	17	27
Honduras	17	25
Canada	17	24
Jamaica	14	24

FACT

Guest teams from other confederations who have played in the CONCACAF Gold Cup include Qatar, South Africa and Brazil.

In 1993, Mexico's Luís Roberto Alves – aka Zague – logged the **most goals in a CONCACAF Gold Cup tournament**, scoring 11 times. His tally included an incredible seven in one game, against Martinique.

YOUNGEST CONCACAF GOLD CUP GOAL SCORER

Canada's Alphonso Davies (b. GHA, 2 Nov 2000) was 16 years 247 days old when he scored twice against French Guiana on 7 Jul 2017. He won the tournament's Golden Boot and Young Player awards. Davies joined Bayern Munich in 2019 and developed into one of the world's most exciting full-backs, nicknamed "Roadrunner" on account of his express pace.

MOST WINS OF THE CONCACAF GOLD CUP

On 6 Jul 2025, Mexico claimed their 10th title, defeating the USA 2–1 in the final at Houston's NRG Stadium. They first lifted the Gold Cup in 1993, the first of three successive triumphs. Mexico's most memorable victory came in 2011, when they stormed back from 2–0 down in the final to beat the USA 4–2. The only other nations to win the tournament are the USA (seven times) and Canada (once, in 2000).

UEFA WOMEN'S EUROPEAN CHAMPIONSHIP

At the first UEFA Women's Euros in 1984 – won by Sweden – the games only lasted 70 min and a smaller size-4 football was used. It's a far cry from the 2025 edition, which saw the continent's top 16 teams do battle across 31 matches, drawing in a total TV audience of more than 400 million.

PLAYER PROFILE

Birgit Prinz

German striker Prinz is the most dominant player in the history of the Women's Euros, winning five tournaments from 1995 to 2009. She made the **most appearances** (23, *see below*) and scored the **most goals** (10 – shared with compatriot Inka Grings). Prinz made her Euros finals debut aged just 17, scoring in the final as Germany beat Sweden 3–2.

MOST WINS OF THE UEFA WOMEN'S EUROS

Germany have won eight of the 14 editions of the Women's Euros. They followed two early triumphs in 1989 and 1991 with six titles in a row between 1995 and 2013. Germany remained champions for 22 years, until a 2–1 loss to Denmark in 2017 ended their streak. They haven't won the Euros since, something that they'll be keen to put right at the next tournament in 2029.

OLDEST GOAL SCORER AT THE UEFA WOMEN'S EUROS

Striker Jess Fishlock (b. 14 Jan 1987) was 38 years 176 days old when she scored for Wales against France in St Gallen, Switzerland, on 9 Jul 2025. Although France won the match 4–1, Wales could still celebrate their first-ever goal at a major women's tournament. Fishlock retired in Oct 2025, having scored 48 times for her country.

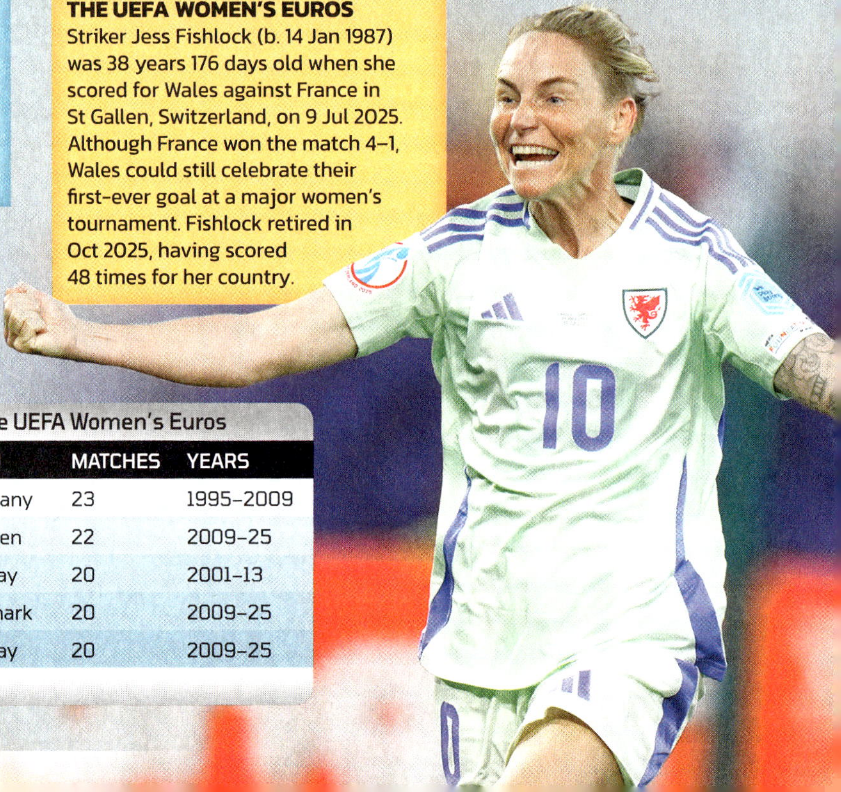

Most games at the UEFA Women's Euros

PLAYER	TEAM	MATCHES	YEARS
Birgit Prinz	Germany	23	1995–2009
Kosovare Asllani (*left*)	Sweden	22	2009–25
Solveig Gulbrandsen	Norway	20	2001–13
Nadia Nadim	Denmark	20	2009–25
Maren Mjelde	Norway	20	2009–25

MOST GAMES WON BY A MANAGER AT THE UEFA WOMEN'S EUROS

Sarina Wiegman (NLD) oversaw 14 victories with the Netherlands and England between 2017 and 2025, winning the tournament three times in a row. She won all six games with the Dutch in 2017 and was present for five of England's six wins in 2022, missing a match due to COVID-19 restrictions. In 2025, England won three of their six games, only beating Sweden and Spain on penalties after the match had finished tied.

The 2025 edition saw the **most goals at a UEFA Women's Euros** – 106. Spain (18 goals) and England (16) led the way – in the final, they drew 1–1 before the Lionesses won on penalties, with Chloe Kelly (*right*) nailing the decisive spot-kick.

657,291

Total spectators at Euro 2025 – the **largest attendance at a UEFA Women's Euros tournament**.

MOST GOAL SCORERS FOR A TEAM AT A UEFA WOMEN'S EUROS

A total of 11 England players found the net at the 2025 tournament in Switzerland. Keira Walsh, Lauren James, Georgia Stanway, Ella Toone, Lauren Hemp, Alessia Russo, Beth Mead, Aggie Beever-Jones, Lucy Bronze, Michelle Agyemang and Chloe Kelly all made it on to the scoresheet. But the Lionesses couldn't beat their own record for the **most goals scored by a team at a UEFA Women's Euros** – 22 – which they had set at the previous edition in 2022.

WOMEN'S AFRICA CUP OF NATIONS

The first African Women's Championship was held in 1991 to determine the qualifiers for the inaugural FIFA Women's World Cup, held that same year. The tournament was renamed the Women's Africa Cup of Nations (WAFCON) in 2015. The latest edition, in 2025, saw teams playing for a new trophy – which was claimed by a familiar winner...

Morocco's Ghizlane Chebbak scored five times in 2025 to finish as top scorer, having won the Best Player award at the previous tournament in 2022.

MOST GOALS AT THE WOMEN'S AFRICA CUP OF NATIONS

Nigerian football icon Perpetua Nkwocha scored 34 times in seven tournaments from 2002 to 2014. She won the competition five times and finished top scorer on four occasions. In the 2004 final against Cameroon, Nkwocha hit the **most goals in a WAFCON match**, scoring four times as Nigeria won 5–0. Her feat was equalled by Asisat Oshoala (NGA) against Mali in 2016.

The 2022 WAFCON tournament was the first to feature 12 teams. Four countries made their debut – Botswana (*left*), Burkina Faso, Burundi and Togo. Botswana, nicknamed the Mares, managed to qualify from the group stages and reach the quarter-finals.

The only teams besides Nigeria to win the WAFCON are Equatorial Guinea (2008 and 2012) and South Africa (2022).

MOST WINS OF THE WOMEN'S AFRICA CUP OF NATIONS

Nigeria claimed their 10th WAFCON title in 13 editions on 26 Jul 2025, following a dramatic 3–2 comeback win over hosts Morocco in Rabat. Midfielder Jennifer Echegini struck the 88th-min winner. Nigeria won five titles in a row between 1998 and 2006, with further triumphs in 2010, 2014, 2016 and 2018. The Super Falcons also won the first two African Women's Championships in 1991 and 1995, but these tournaments are not usually included in official WAFCON statistics.

COPA AMÉRICA FEMENINA

There have been 10 editions of the South American women's championship since 1991. Brazil have dominated the tournament, winning every title bar 2006, when they lost out to Argentina. But with the FIFA Women's World Cup coming to South America for the first time in 2027, the competition is definitely hotting up.

MOST WINS OF THE COPA AMÉRICA FEMENINA
On 2 Aug 2025, Brazil claimed their ninth title in thrilling fashion, edging Colombia 5–4 on penalties in Quito, Ecuador. A seesawing game had finished 4–4; Brazil legend Marta came off the bench to score an equalizer deep into injury time, before striking again in extra time (*below*). Goalkeeper Lorena was the hero in the shootout, saving the decisive Colombian penalty.

FACT

Marta retired after the 2024 Olympics, only to return – at the age of 39 – for the 2025 Copa América Femenina. Her haul of three goals and three assists earned her the Golden Ball award.

YOUNGEST TOP GOAL SCORER AT THE COPA AMÉRICA FEMENINA
Paraguay's Claudia Martínez (b. 15 Jan 2008) was aged 17 years 199 days at the conclusion of the 2025 tournament, when she finished joint top scorer alongside Brazil's Amanda Gutierres. Martínez struck six times in five games, scoring a hat-trick against Bolivia on her finals debut. She followed up with strikes against Colombia, Brazil and Venezuela.

In 2025, Chile extended their shared record with Brazil for the **most Copa América Femenina tournament appearances** to 10. They are the only teams to feature in every edition to date.

ROUND-UP

As the game continues to grow around the world, new competitions are springing up to take their place alongside established continental tournaments. The Nations League has proved a particular hit with fans, replacing many international friendlies.

MOST WINS OF THE OFC MEN'S NATIONS CUP

A tournament to decide the men's champions of Oceania has been running since 1973. On 30 Jun 2024, New Zealand claimed their sixth title, overcoming co-hosts Vanuatu 3–0 in Port Vila. The All Whites won all four of their matches, scoring 15 goals and conceding none. Their closest rivals are Australia, who won four Nations Cups before leaving the OFC for the Asian Football Confederation in 2006.

Wonder Wood
On 9 Sep 2025, New Zealand striker Chris Wood edged ahead in the race to become the OFC's all-time highest scorer, notching his 45th international goal during a 3–1 defeat in the "Soccer Ashes" against Australia. Wood moved one goal clear of Fiji's Roy Krishna.

MOST WINS OF THE UEFA WOMEN'S NATIONS LEAGUE

Spain have won both editions to date of this new European competition. They defended their 2023/24 title in style in 2025, winning eight of their 10 matches and seeing off Germany 3–0 over two legs in the final. Spain's 3–0 second-leg victory was only their second-ever win against Germany, with the first coming in the semi-finals of the 2025 UEFA Women's Euros.

Spain striker Clàudia Pina scored twice in the Nations League final second leg to finish the tournament as joint-top scorer with eight goals, alongside Belgium's Tessa Wullaert.

MOST WINS OF THE CONCACAF W CHAMPIONSHIP

On 18 Jul 2022, the USA beat Canada 1–0 via an Alex Morgan penalty to claim their ninth continental crown for North and Central America and the Caribbean. The USA have lost only one match across the 10 tournaments in which they have participated, a 2–1 defeat to Mexico in 2010. Canada lifted the trophy that year and also triumphed in 1998, when the USA did not participate.

MOST WINS OF THE AFRICAN NATIONS CHAMPIONSHIP

Commonly known as CHAN, this biennial tournament was open only to domestic-based players. Following previous wins in 2018 and 2020, Morocco won a record third title in 2025, overcoming Madagascar 3–2 in the final. This was the final CHAN tournament, with the competition set to be replaced by the African Nations League from 2029.

PRIDE OF CANADA

Canada's Jonathan David has scored eight times in the CONCACAF Nations League, including the winner in the third place play-off against the USA on 23 Mar 2025. The Juventus star became Canada's all-time top scorer on 19 Nov 2024 and now has 39 goals for *Les Rouges*.

MOST WINS OF THE CONCACAF NATIONS LEAGUE

The USA have won three of the four CONCACAF Nations League competitions held to date, triumphing in 2021 and 2023–24. They secured their most recent title with a 2–0 victory over Mexico, thanks to goals from Tyler Adams and Giovanni Reyna. The USA's winning streak ended in the 2025 semi-finals, when they suffered a last-gasp 1–0 defeat to Panama.

FEATURE

INTERNATIONAL LEGENDS

To play just once for your country is an incredible honour. But the players on this page have taken national service to a new level, turning out year after year and representing their homelands in competitions and tournaments around the world.

The "Queen of Caps" Kristine Lilly played 354 times for the USA between 1987 and 2010 – the **most women's international matches**. She won the 1999 FIFA World Cup and two Olympic gold medals. Lilly's total includes the **most matches played at the FIFA Women's World Cup** – 30.

MOST WOMEN'S INTERNATIONAL MATCHES PLAYED

NAME	TEAM	FIRST CAP	LAST CAP	MATCHES
Kristine Lilly	USA	3 Aug 1987	5 Nov 2010	354
Christine Sinclair	Canada	12 Mar 2000	5 Dec 2023	331
Carli Lloyd	USA	10 Jul 2005	26 Oct 2021	316
Christie Pearce	USA	28 Feb 1997	20 Sep 2015	311
Mia Hamm	USA	3 Aug 1987	8 Dec 2004	276
Julie Foudy	USA	29 Jul 1988	8 Dec 2004	274
Abby Wambach	USA	9 Sep 2001	16 Dec 2015	255
Sherida Spitse	Netherlands	31 Aug 2006	28 Oct 2025	248
Joy Fawcett	USA	3 Aug 1987	26 Aug 2004	241
Caroline Seger	Sweden	9 Mar 2005	31 Oct 2023	240

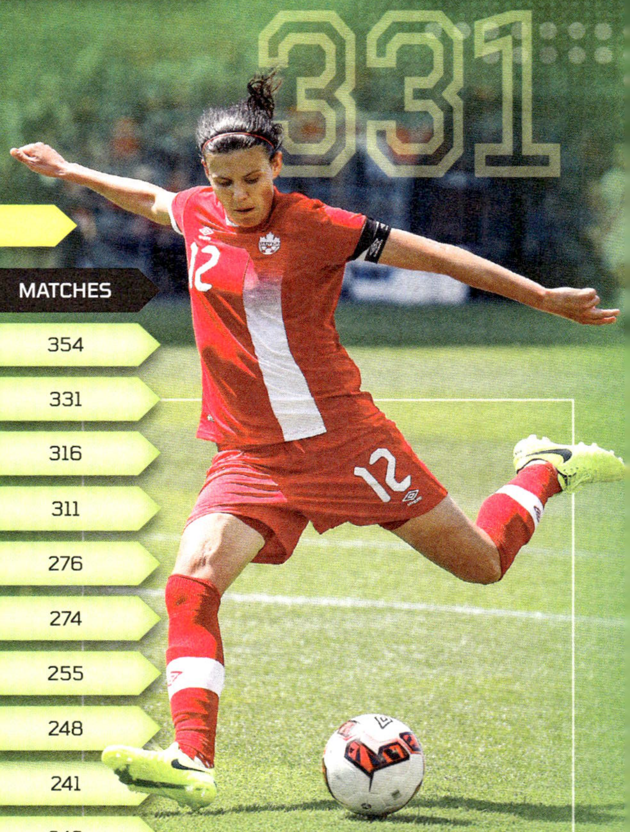

Canada striker Christine Sinclair scored the **most goals in women's international football**, hitting 190 in her 331 matches. She played at six FIFA World Cups, amassing the **most matches played as captain** at the tournament – 18.

Cristiano Ronaldo (PRT) has played the **most men's international matches** – 233. He received a GWR certificate before his 200th game, a 1–0 win over Iceland on 20 Jun 2023. Ronaldo has also scored the **most international goals** – 146 – netting at least once for 23 consecutive years since 2004.

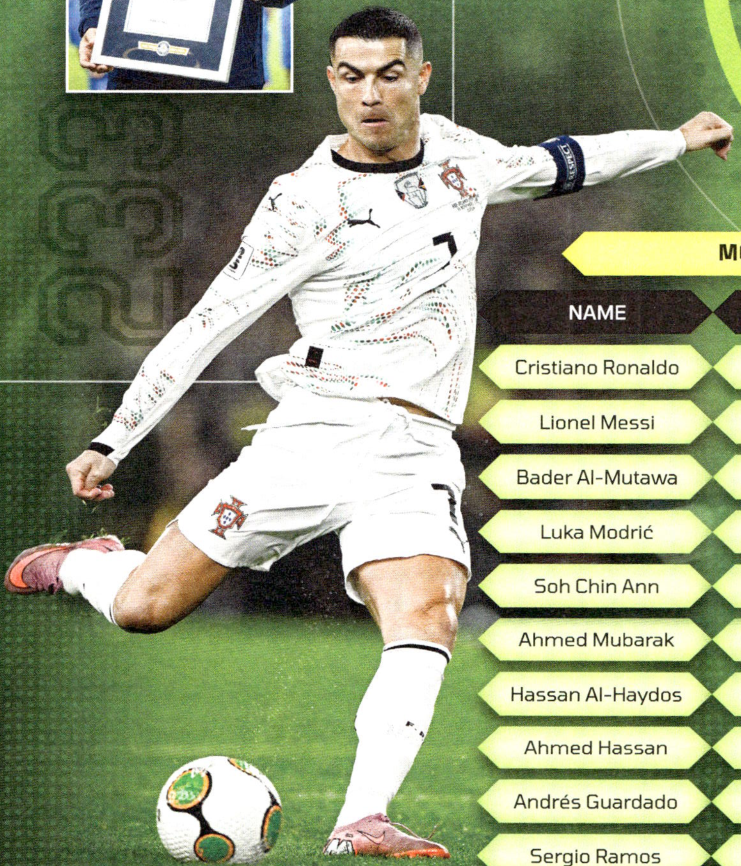

Centre-back Sergio Ramos racked up 180 games for Spain, winning the 2010 FIFA World Cup and two UEFA European Championships. He also scored the **most men's international goals by a defender** – 23.

Kuwait's Bader Al-Mutawa held the men's international appearance record twice: upon gaining his 185th cap on 25 Jun 2021, and his 196th and final cap the following year. His total was later adjusted to 202.

MOST MEN'S INTERNATIONAL MATCHES PLAYED

NAME	TEAM	FIRST CAP	LAST CAP	MATCHES
Cristiano Ronaldo	Portugal	20 Aug 2003	6 Jul 2026	233
Lionel Messi	Argentina	17 Aug 2005	19 Jul 2026	207
Bader Al-Mutawa	Kuwait	4 Sep 2003	14 Jun 2022	202
Luka Modrić	Croatia	1 Mar 2006	2 Jul 2026	202
Soh Chin Ann	Malaysia	19 Nov 1969	18 Oct 1984	195
Ahmed Mubarak	Oman	25 Sep 2003	2 Dec 2019	193
Hassan Al-Haydos	Qatar	9 Aug 2008	24 Jun 2026	189
Ahmed Hassan	Egypt	29 Dec 1995	22 May 2012	183
Andrés Guardado	Mexico	14 Dec 2005	15 Oct 2024	180
Sergio Ramos	Spain	26 Mar 2005	31 Mar 2021	180

WORLD TOURNAMENTS

The first "football world championships" was held in 1888, when Scottish Cup winners Renton beat English FA Cup holders West Bromwich Albion 4–1. As the game took hold around the world, so international tournaments became truly global. The first FIFA World Cup took place in 1930; the first official women's tournament arrived in 1991. A total of 209 nations entered qualifying for the 2026 FIFA World Cup, which with 48 teams became the largest yet.

MOST GOALS AT A FIFA WOMEN'S WORLD CUP TOURNAMENT

A total of 164 goals were scored at the 2023 World Cup in Australia and New Zealand. Every team found the net at least once – bar Haiti and Vietnam – while Spain hit 18. Japan's Hinata Miyazawa scored five times to top the individual standings and claim the Golden Boot. The final goal of the tournament was fired home by Spain captain Olga Carmona, earning her country a 1–0 victory over England and their first FIFA Women's World Cup triumph (*above*).

CONTENTS

Australia star Sam Kerr scored one of the goals of the 2023 FIFA Women's World Cup, spectacularly firing home from distance in the semi-final against England.

FIFA WORLD CUP

With an expanded line-up of 48 teams, the 2026 tournament was the largest yet, with the **most matches at a FIFA World Cup** – 104. The battle for the greatest prize in football didn't disappoint, with a series of classic matches and a slew of records falling.

SMALLEST COUNTRY BY POPULATION AT THE FIFA WORLD CUP

The Caribbean island of Curaçao qualified for the tournament in 2026 despite having a population of just 156,000 people. Curaçao drew on its historic ties to the Netherlands to field a team drawn largely from former Dutch youth internationals. The "Blue Wave" won new fans from around the world with their heroic displays, earning their first FIFA World Cup point with a 0–0 draw against Ecuador. Gilbert Martina, President of the Curaçao Football Federation, was presented with a GWR certificate by Adjudicator Hannah Ortman on 15 Jun 2026 (*inset*).

MOST FIFA WORLD CUP TOURNAMENTS SCORED IN

Cristiano Ronaldo (PRT) struck in six consecutive tournaments for Portugal between 2006 and 2026. He hit a brace against Uzbekistan on 23 Jun 2026 to reclaim the outright record, after his previous total of five had been equalled by Lionel Messi. At the age of 41, Ronaldo became the second-oldest scorer in World Cup history, behind Cameroon's Roger Milla (42 years 39 days, in 1994).

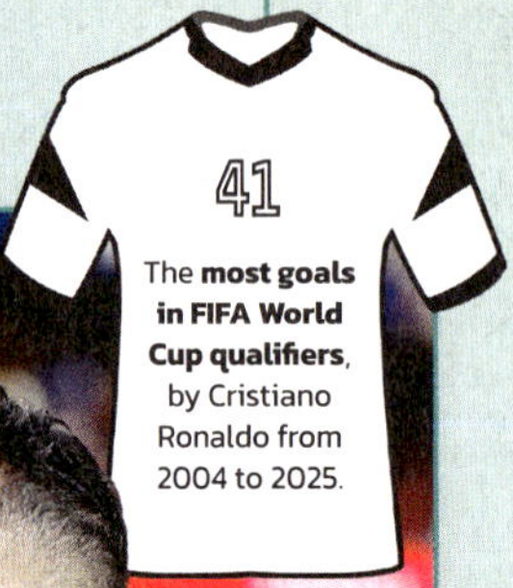

The **most goals in FIFA World Cup qualifiers**, by Cristiano Ronaldo from 2004 to 2025.

Germany's Manuel Neuer has played the **most matches by a goalkeeper at the FIFA World Cup** – 23. He featured at five tournaments between 2010 and 2026, keeping a clean sheet in the 2014 final against Argentina. Neuer overtook Hugo Lloris's record of 20 games between the sticks during the group stages of the 2026 tournament, before Germany crashed out on penalties to Paraguay in the Round of 32.

MOST FIFA WORLD CUP TOURNAMENT APPEARANCES

Brazil are the only team to have played at all 23 World Cups – two more than their closest rivals, Germany. In 2026, Brazil reached the Round of 16, extending their all-time records for the **most games played** (119), **most matches won** (79) and **most goals scored** (247). Although success has eluded the *Seleçao* in recent years, they remain World Cup royalty and can still boast the **most wins of the FIFA World Cup** – five.

Erling Haaland was unstoppable on his tournament debut, scoring seven goals in five matches for Norway. The Scandinavian side became famous for their "Viking Row" celebration, which saw them and thousands of fans pull on invisible oars at the same time while shouting "Ro!".

OLDEST GOALKEEPER TO KEEP A CLEAN SHEET ON FIFA WORLD CUP DEBUT

Vozinha (b. 3 Jun 1986) was 40 years 12 days old when his Cape Verde side held Spain to a 0–0 draw on 15 Jun 2026. He made seven saves to keep the European champions at bay. The third-smallest nation in tournament history, Cape Verde qualified for the knockout round and gave Argentina a scare before going down to a dramatic 3–2 defeat after extra time.

MOST PENALTIES SCORED AT THE FIFA WORLD CUP

Harry Kane has converted six spot-kicks for England in tournament play, excluding shootouts. He gained sole ownership of the record in 2026, with successful penalties against Croatia and Mexico. Kane has a conversion rate of 85%, with just a solitary miss against France in 2022.

FIFA WORLD CUP

MOST GOALS SCORED AT A FIFA WORLD CUP TOURNAMENT

A total of 308 goals were recorded in 2026, smashing the previous best of 172 from 2022. This was largely due to the expanded format, which increased the number of games by 40. The 2026 haul included the **most own goals** – 14 – and the **most goals by substitutes** – 59. The highest scorers were England (*above*) and France, who both netted 20 times.

Didier Deschamps (FRA) oversaw the **most FIFA World Cup matches by a manager** – 26 – across four tournaments. He guided France to a quarter-final, a semi-final and two finals. France's victory in 2018 made Deschamps only the third person, after Mário Zagallo and Franz Beckenbauer, to win the World Cup as both a player and a coach.

The **most assists at a FIFA World Cup tournament** is 7, by Michael Olise (FRA) across eight games in 2026. The English-born midfielder overtook Pelé's record of six assists in 1970 by setting up two goals during France's 6–4 defeat to England in the bronze-medal match. Five of Olise's seven assists were for striker Kylian Mbappé (*see opposite*).

The 2026 World Cup averaged 2.96 goals per game. The **highest goal average at a FIFA World Cup** is 5.38, at Switzerland 1954. There were 140 goals in just 26 matches!

MOST FIFA WORLD CUP MATCHES PLAYED

Lionel Messi appeared in 34 games for Argentina, winning 23 of them. He made his World Cup debut in 2006 and featured in a record-equalling six tournaments. Messi reached three finals, memorably lifting the trophy in 2022. He scored 21 World Cup goals – 15 of them after he had turned 35!

In 2026, Messi (b. 24 Jun 1987) became the **oldest player to score a hat-trick at the FIFA World Cup**, aged 38 years 357 days, against Algeria. He also racked up the **most consecutive FIFA World Cup matches scored in** – 9.

LONGEST FIFA WORLD CUP CLEAN SHEET

Spain goalkeeper Unai Simón didn't concede a tournament goal for 650 min across two World Cups between 2022 and 2026. His historic shutout run started in the second half of Spain's 2–1 loss to Japan in Qatar. In 2026, Spain didn't concede a goal in their first five matches, before Belgium's Charles De Ketelaere scored in the 41st min of their quarter-final tie. Simón beat the previous record of 518 min, set by Italy's Walter Zenga in 1990.

MOST GOALS SCORED AT THE FIFA WORLD CUP

Kylian Mbappé (FRA) scored 22 times in 22 games across three World Cup tournaments. The deadly marksman overtook Lionel Messi's total of 21 goals with a brace against England in the 2026 bronze-medal match. Mbappé became the first player to win the Golden Boot twice, scoring eight times in 2022 and 10 in 2026. His total also includes the **most goals in FIFA World Cup finals** – four (*see p.153*).

LONGEST UNBEATEN RUN IN MEN'S INTERNATIONALS

Spain went 38 games without defeat between 26 Mar 2024 and 19 Jul 2026. They won both the UEFA European Championship and the FIFA World Cup in this period, overtaking Italy's record of 37 in the World Cup final against Argentina – which Spain won 1–0 after extra time, thanks to a goal from substitute Ferran Torres (*below, third from left*). *La Roja* had been unstoppable throughout the tournament, conceding just one goal in eight matches.

Spain's captain Rodri made the **most completed passes at a FIFA World Cup tournament** – 790 – in 2026.

FIFA WOMEN'S WORLD CUP

The first FIFA-recognized Women's World Cup took place in 1991, when 12 teams battled it out in China. There have been a further eight editions since, with the most recent held in Australia and New Zealand in 2023 – the first Southern Hemisphere tournament, it also featured an expanded roster of 32 sides.

Canadian striker Christine Sinclair made the **most FIFA Women's World Cup appearances as captain**, skippering Les Rouges in 18 matches. She scored 10 times across a total of six tournaments from 2003 to 2023.

LONGEST PENALTY SHOOTOUT AT THE FIFA WOMEN'S WORLD CUP

Following a 0–0 draw between Australia and France on 12 Aug 2023, the teams settled their quarter-final with an epic contest from 12 yards out. After 19 spot-kicks, Cortnee Vine stepped up and netted for the Matildas to win the shootout 7–6, breaking French hearts.

Most goals at the FIFA Women's World Cup

PLAYER	TEAM	GOALS	TOURNAMENTS
Marta	Brazil	17	2003–23
Birgit Prinz	Germany	14	1995–2011
Abby Wambach	USA	14	2003–15
Michelle Akers	USA	12	1991–99
Sun Wen	China	11	1991–2003
Bettina Wiegmann	Germany	11	1991–2003
Cristiane	Brazil	11	2003–19

Marta reached 17 World Cup goals with a penalty against Italy in 2019. She played in 23 games at six tournaments.

Brazil's Formiga (b. 3 Mar 1978) made the **most FIFA Women's World Cup tournament appearances**, featuring in seven editions from 1995 to 2019. She was 41 years 112 days old at the time of her final game on 23 Jun 2019, making her also the tournament's **oldest player**.

MOST GOALS IN A FIFA WOMEN'S WORLD CUP FINAL

Carli Lloyd (USA) scored a hat-trick during the USA's 5–2 defeat of Japan on 5 Jul 2015. She netted three times in the opening 16 min, completing her hat-trick with a stunning lob of the Japanese keeper from the halfway line. Lloyd struck in six successive games across the 2015 and 2019 tournaments – the **most consecutive FIFA Women's World Cup matches scored in**.

MOST WINS OF THE FIFA WOMEN'S WORLD CUP

The USA are four-time women's world champions. They claimed the first-ever title in 1991 in China, powered by Michelle Akers' tournament-record 10 goals. Eight years later, on home soil, the USA defeated China on penalties to lift the trophy before a 90,000-strong crowd. They romped home in Canada in 2015 (*see above*) and secured back-to-back wins four years later with a series of dominant displays in France.

The USA went on the rampage in 2019, scoring the **most goals at a FIFA Women's World Cup tournament** – 26. They thumped Thailand 13–0!

FIFA CLUB WORLD CUP

The idea of a competition to find the best club side in the world has existed since the early 20th century. The first official FIFA Club World Cup was held in 2000 and was won by Brazil's Corinthians. In 2025, the tournament expanded to 32 teams – Chelsea emerged triumphant, beating Paris Saint-Germain 3–0 in the final.

HIGHEST MARGIN OF VICTORY IN A FIFA CLUB WORLD CUP MATCH
On 15 Jun 2025, Bayern Munich (DEU) thrashed Auckland City 10–0 at TQL Stadium in Cincinnati, Ohio, USA. The German champions were too strong for the New Zealand amateur outfit, who were 6–0 down at half-time. Jamal Musiala (DEU) came off the bench to score a hat-trick, equalling the record for the **most goals in a FIFA Club World Cup match** (*see p.34*).

MOST WINS OF THE FIFA CLUB WORLD CUP
Real Madrid (ESP) have claimed five titles in seven tournament appearances. They came fourth in 2000 and made the semi-finals in 2025.

Former Real star Toni Kroos (DEU, *standing third from right*) has the **most wins by a player** – six. Five of these came with Madrid, and he also lifted the trophy with Bayern Munich in 2013.

TEAM	TITLES	YEARS
Real Madrid (ESP)	5	2014, 2016–18, 2022
Barcelona (ESP)	3	2009, 2011, 2015
Corinthians (BRA)	2	2000, 2012
Bayern Munich (DEU)	2	2013, 2020
Chelsea (UK)	2	2021, 2025

Most goals at the FIFA Club World Cup
Cristiano Ronaldo (PRT) is the competition's all-time top scorer with seven goals. He struck once in 2008, as Manchester United claimed their only Club World Cup. Four more goals followed in 2016, with Real Madrid, when Ronaldo became the first player to hit a hat-trick in the final. He added two more goals in 2017.

Ramos wore the no.93 shirt for Monterrey to mark his 93rd-min goal in the 2014 UEFA Champions League final.

OLDEST GOAL SCORER AT THE FIFA CLUB WORLD CUP

Sergio Ramos (ESP, b. 30 Mar 1986) was 39 years 79 days old when he found the net for Mexican side Monterrey during their 1–1 draw against Inter Milan on 17 Jun 2025. The veteran defender claimed the record from former Inter stalwart Javier Zanetti, who scored against Seongnam FC in 2010 at the age of 37 years 127 days.

Egyptian winger Hussein El Shahat extended his record for the **most FIFA Club World Cup matches** to 18 with three appearances for Al Ahly in 2025. It was his sixth tournament in total. He reached the final in 2018, playing for the UAE's Al Ain.

YOUNG GUN

On 13 Dec 2006, Alexandre Pato (BRA, b. 2 Sep 1989) became the **youngest goal scorer at the FIFA Club World Cup**, striking for Brazilian side Internacional against Al Ahly aged 17 years 102 days. It was only Pato's second-ever professional game. He became the youngest player to score in any senior FIFA men's competition, breaking the record set by Pelé at the 1958 World Cup by 137 days.

OLYMPIC FOOTBALL

Men's football has been on the Olympic programme at every Games bar two – 1896 and 1932. Currently, only players under the age of 23 are eligible to play, with three exceptions per squad. The first Olympic women's football tournament didn't take place until 1996, with no restrictions placed on selections.

MOST OLYMPIC MEN'S FOOTBALL TITLES

Great Britain and Hungary have both won gold three times. Great Britain's first triumph came in 1900, when they were represented by amateur English side Upton Park FC. They followed up with wins in 1908 and 1912. Hungary claimed their first title in 1952, part of a 31-game unbeaten streak. The Magyars also claimed Olympic gold in 1964 (*above*) and 1968.

MOST GOALS IN OLYMPIC WOMEN'S FOOTBALL

Brazil striker Cristiane struck 14 times across four Games. She finished top scorer in both 2004 and 2008, claiming a silver medal both times. Her total includes a lightning-quick hat-trick against Nigeria, which she completed in just 15 min.

MOST GOALS BY A TEAM IN AN OLYMPIC WOMEN'S FOOTBALL TOURNAMENT

The Netherlands went goal crazy at the delayed 2020 Summer Games in Japan, smashing in 23 goals in just four matches. Ten of these were scored by Vivianne Miedema (*left, centre*), who claimed the **individual** tournament goal record. The Dutch thrashed Zambia 10–3 and China 8–2 in the group stages, also drawing 3–3 with Brazil. They were knocked out on penalties in the quarter-finals, following a 2–2 draw with the USA.

OLDEST GOAL SCORER IN OLYMPIC MEN'S FOOTBALL

Ryan Giggs (UK, b. 29 Nov 1973) was 38 years 243 days old when he headed home for Team GB against the UAE at London's Wembley Stadium on 29 Jul 2012. The Manchester United winger was captain of a team comprised of English and Welsh players. It was the first time that a men's Great Britain football team had competed at the Olympics since 1960. They reached the quarter-finals, losing on penalties to South Korea.

Deanne Rose (b. 3 Mar 1999) is the **youngest goal scorer in Olympic women's football**, netting for Canada against Brazil aged 17 years 169 days on 19 Aug 2016.

FASTEST GOAL IN OLYMPIC MEN'S FOOTBALL

On 17 Aug 2016, Neymar scored for Brazil after just 14 sec of play in their semi-final against Honduras. His early strike set Brazil on their way to a 6–0 victory at Rio's Maracanã Stadium. Brazil went on to seal an emotional first-ever Olympic triumph, beating Germany on penalties in the final.

MOST OLYMPIC WOMEN'S FOOTBALL TITLES

The USA have won five of the eight Olympic women's football competitions held to date. They became the inaugural gold medallists at Atlanta 1996, defeating China 2–1 in the final. Between 2004 and 2012, the USA claimed three Olympic titles in a row, before suffering a shock exit to Sweden in the 2016 quarter-finals. They returned to the top of the podium at the 2024 Games in Paris (*below*), winning all six of their matches.

ROUND-UP

The global game can assume many forms. There are FIFA tournaments played indoors and on sand, while the Paralympics offers a platform for players with disabilities to show off their skills. However, whatever the format, one particular nation has a habit of finishing ahead of the competition...

MOST WINS OF THE FIFA BEACH SOCCER WORLD CUP

On 11 May 2025, Brazil claimed their seventh World Cup title on sand, defeating Belarus 4–3 in the Seychelles. Two goals from Golden Ball winner Rodrigo helped the Seleção on their way. The first FIFA Beach Soccer World Cup was held in 2005; Brazil won four tournaments in a row between 2006 and 2009, and also triumphed in 2017 and 2024.

In 2025, Seychelles star Lienal Bibi (*above*) struck twice against Japan, aged 16 years 259 days, to become the third-youngest scorer ever at the FIFA Beach Soccer World Cup. The **youngest goal scorer** outright is Abu Azeez (b. 31 May 1994), who was 15 years 170 days old when he scored for Nigeria on 17 Nov 2009.

Most goals at the FIFA Beach Soccer World Cup

PLAYER	TEAM	GAMES	GOALS
Madjer	Portugal	49	88
Dejan Stankovic	Switzerland	27	47
Gabriele Gori	Italy	22	41
Belchior	Portugal	48	39
Bruno	Brazil	37	39

In 2016, Madjer made history by becoming the first player to score 1,000 international beach soccer goals.

TOP OF THE WORLD

Club football has two new intercontinental champions. The second men's FIFA Intercontinental Cup was claimed by Paris Saint-Germain on 17 Dec 2025 (*above*). The European champions defeated Brazil's Flamengo on penalties after their final in Al Rayyan, Qatar, ended 1–1.

In 2026, the continental champions of the women's game were pitted against one another in the FIFA Champions Cup. Arsenal (*left*) overcame Corinthians 3–2 in the final on 1 Feb to pocket a cool £1.7 m ($2.3 m).

In 2025, Brazil won the first-ever indoor FIFA Futsal Women's World Cup. They won all six of their games in the Philippines, defeating Portugal 3–0 in the final on 7 Dec. On the scoresheet was Amandinha (*above, far right*), winner of the **most futsal Best Women's Player in the World awards** – eight, between 2014 and 2021.

MOST PARALYMPIC BLIND FOOTBALL TITLES

Brazil won the first five editions of the Paralympic blind, or five-a-side, football event between 2004 and 2021. They claimed bronze at Paris 2024, losing on penalties to Argentina in the semi-final. Players wear eye shades and have to listen out for the noise-making device inside the ball and shouted prompts from guides.

FEATURE

ALTERNATIVE KICKS

Tired of playing the same old matches? Looking for a new way to express your skills? Check out these weird and wonderful variations on the beautiful game...

A line-up of soccer legends including Lionel Messi built their own footvolley court for a 2009 Pepsi advert.

FOOTVOLLEY

Originating on the beaches of Rio de Janeiro in Brazil in the 1960s, footvolley gives players the chance to show off their soccer skills on the sand. Signature moves include the "shark attack", where the ball is struck over the 2.2-m-high (7-ft) net with a head-high volley. Brazil's Romário is one of a number of famous footballers who honed their skills playing footvolley.

TEQBALL

The brainchild of a trio of Hungarian football fans, this mash-up of soccer and table tennis has enjoyed a rapid rise in popularity. Players face off across a curved table, and are allowed three touches to return the ball over the net. FIFA World Cup winner Ronaldinho has acted as a global ambassador for the sport. A Teqball World Championships has been held annually since 2017.

FOOTGOLF

In this cross between football and golf, players have to reach the green zone from the teeing zone in as few kicks as possible. The hole has a diameter of 50 cm (1 ft 7 in) in order to accommodate a size-5 soccer ball. Footgolf was created in the Netherlands in 2008. Professional footgolfers include ex-Liverpool striker Florent Sinama Pongolle (*inset*).

CYCLE-BALL

Popular in European countries such as Germany, Austria and Czechia, this game is contested by teams of two riding fixed-gear bicycles with no brakes. Players try to score in the opposition's goal while in the saddle, using either their body or the front or back wheel to strike the ball. The first World Cycle-Ball Championships were held in 1930.

SEPAK TAKRAW

A south-east Asian sport that combines elements of football, volleyball and martial arts, sepak takraw is an explosive and acrobatic spectacle. Competitors use their feet to volley a plastic or rattan ball over a net. Thailand have claimed the **most sepak takraw team regu titles at the Asian Games**, having won seven men's tournaments and six women's to date.

SWAMP FOOTBALL

This begrimed version of the beautiful game began as summer training for Finnish cross-country skiers. Matches are played on a 35 x 60-m (114 x 196-ft) quagmire, with sides made up of a goalkeeper and five outfield players. Teams pledge an "Oath of the Swamp" beforehand, vowing to honour nature and respect the opposition. The **longest-running annual swamp soccer tournament** is the Swamp Soccer World Championships, first held in 2000 in Hyrynsalmi, Finland.

FIFA WORLD CUP CLASSICS

In celebration of the 2026 FIFA World Cup, we put together our list of the 20 greatest matches in the preceding 22 tournaments. These games have it all: shocking scorelines and surprises, unforgettable moments of drama and skill, red cards and last-minute winners. At the end of our countdown, you'll find a round-up of infamous World Cup encounters that are remembered for all the wrong reasons...

CONTENTS

PICTURE PERFECT
In the 2022 FIFA World Cup final, Lionel Messi cemented his legacy as one of the game's greats by leading Argentina to their third title. In the aftermath of a dramatic victory over France in Lusail, Qatar (*see pp.152–53*), Messi was photographed raising the World Cup trophy over his head. The picture became the **most liked image post on Instagram**, racking up an incredible 74,720,726 hearts. Another snap of Messi in bed with the trophy earned 53 million likes.

A total of 1,068 FIFA World Cup matches had been played across 23 tournaments as of 2026. The shortest edition was Italy 1934, when just 17 games were staged.

20

3 Jul 1994

ROMANIA 3–2 ARGENTINA

Rose Bowl, Pasadena, USA

Dumitrescu 11, 18
Hagi 58

Batistuta 16 (pen.)
Balbo 75

★★★★★

PLAYER PROFILE

Gheorghe Hagi

Widely regarded as Romania's greatest-ever footballer, Hagi (*right, in yellow*) scored 35 times in 124 games for *Tricolorii* ("the Tricolours"). A playmaker blessed with touch and vision, he earned the nickname "Maradona of the Carpathians" and was nominated for the Ballon d'Or six times. Hagi played for both Real Madrid and Barcelona in the 1990s, and won four Turkish league titles with Galatasaray.

19

5 Jun 1938

BRAZIL 6
POLAND 5

Stade de la Meinau, Strasbourg, France

Leônidas 18, 93, 104
Romeu 25
Perácio 44, 71

Scherfke 23 (pen.)
Wilimowski
53, 59, 89, 118

Just 13,000 fans were present in Strasbourg to witness this high-scoring thriller. Playing in their first-ever World Cup match, underdogs Poland pushed Brazil to the limit. On a muddy pitch churned up by rain, they came back from 3–1 to reach full-time level at 4–4. Brazil striker Leônidas (*above, third from left*) scored twice in extra-time to complete his hat-trick and put the game beyond reach. Yet he was eclipsed by Ernst Wilimowski, who struck four times for Poland in his one and only World Cup game.

This pulsating Round-of-16 encounter would have graced any final. Playing without a recognized striker, Romania scored twice early on through Ilie Dumitrescu (*above*) – the second a cool finish from a sublime Gheorghe Hagi pass. Argentina were reeling from the expulsion of Diego Maradona from the tournament, but they still had Gabriel Batistuta, who won and converted a penalty. After the break, Hagi put Romania 3–1 up. Argentina pulled another goal back through Abel Balbo to set up a nail-biting finish, but couldn't conjure up an equalizer.

TEAM FORMATIONS

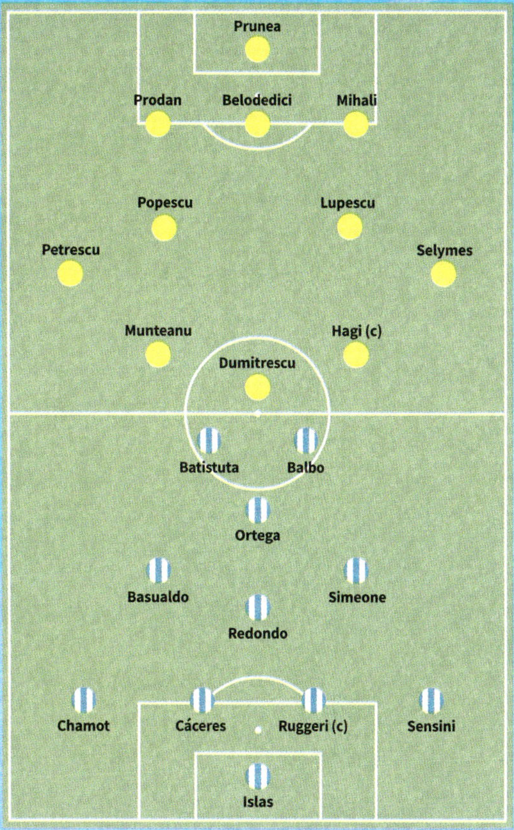

TEAM FORMATIONS

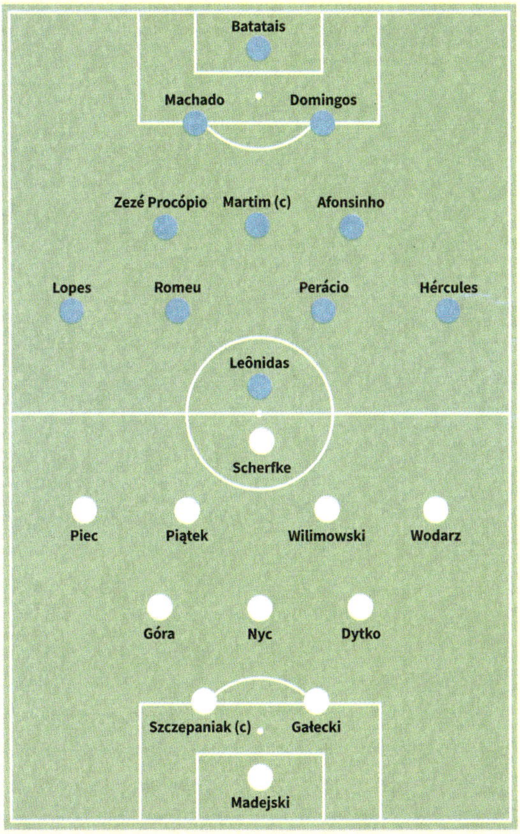

MOST FIFA WORLD CUP GOALS BY A PLAYER ON THE LOSING SIDE

Poland's Ernst Wilimowski scored four times against Brazil and was also felled for the penalty that was converted by teammate Friedrich Scherfke. A pacy, two-footed striker, Wilimowski was renowned for his dribbling skills and prolific scoring. When World War II began, he switched allegiance to Germany and played eight games for them in 1941–42, forever tarnishing his reputation in Poland.

FACT

In Brazil's next match against Czechoslovakia, striker Leônidas hit the headlines by attempting a bicycle kick. One of the earliest players to perform the move, he is often credited with inventing it.

18

4 Jul 1998

NETHERLANDS 2–1 ARGENTINA

Stade Vélodrome, Marseille, France

Netherlands	Argentina
Kluivert 12 Bergkamp 90	López 17

This quarter-final between two World Cup heavyweights saw two red cards and one of the great late winning goals. A striker's finish from Patrick Kluivert put the Netherlands into an early lead, but Argentina struck back through Claudio López. As the tension mounted, Arthur Numan received a second yellow card and Ariel Ortega saw red after a confrontation with the Dutch keeper. Extra time was looming, but Dennis Bergkamp had other ideas. With just three glorious touches, he controlled a long pass from Frank de Boer, turned the defender and fired into the top corner of the net – sealing victory in the most dramatic fashion possible.

"The goal against Argentina is my top goal. To score like that, in my style, on that stage... (Dennis Bergkamp)"

17

31 May 2002

FRANCE 0 SENEGAL 1

Seoul World Cup Stadium, South Korea

Bouba Diop 30

Senegal celebrated Papa Bouba Diop's goal in style, dancing around the no.19's shirt on the ground. "It's something that nobody in Senegal will ever forget," Diop said later.

The opening game of 2002 witnessed one of the greatest upsets in tournament history, as Senegal beat the defending champions in their first-ever World Cup match. France were missing Zinedine Zidane through injury, but still had a team packed with superstars. Yet from kick-off they were overwhelmed by Senegal, whose enterprise and energy was personified by striker El Hadji Diouf. With half an hour gone, he broke free from the French defence and crossed into the box, where Papa Bouba Diop (*above*) bundled home. Despite French pressure, the one goal proved to be enough, and the Lions of Teranga celebrated a remarkable victory.

Rowdy Rematch

In 2022, Argentina and the Netherlands faced off for the sixth time at the World Cup. The ill-tempered game in Lusail, Qatar, saw the **most yellow cards in a FIFA World Cup match** – 18. The bookings included the Argentina manager and coach, while Dutch player Denzel Dumfries received two to earn himself a red card. Argentina won the "Battle of Lusail" on penalties after the game ended 2–2.

TEAM FORMATIONS

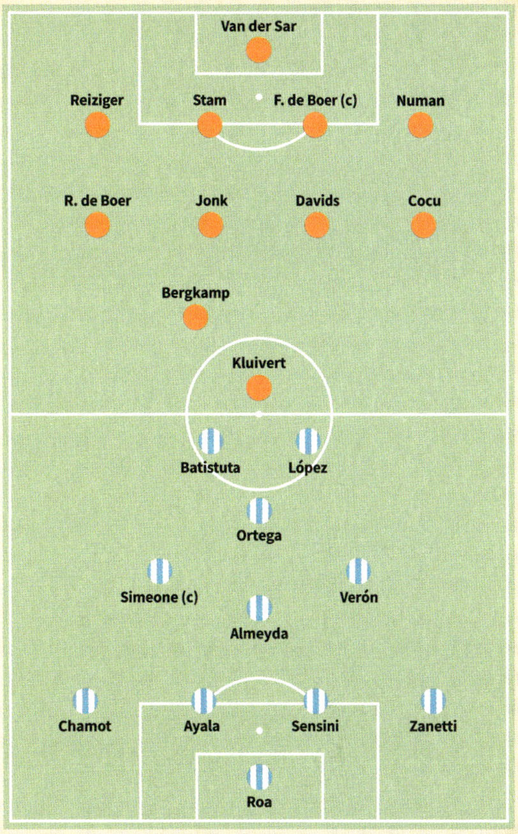

TEAM FORMATIONS

Lions' Pride

Senegal progressed unbeaten from Group A, despite letting a 3–0 lead slip against Uruguay in their final match. A golden goal from Henri Camara dispatched Sweden in the Round of 16, only for the Lions of Teranga to suffer the reverse fate against Türkiye in the quarter-finals. Defending world and European champions France finished bottom of Group A, with one draw and two defeats.

16

15 Jun 1986

SOVIET UNION 3–4 BELGIUM

Estadio Nou Camp, León, Mexico

Soviet Union	Belgium
Belanov 27, 70, 111 (pen.)	Scifo 56 Ceulemans 77 Demol 102 Claesen 110

This Round-of-16 tie saw Belgium spring a spectacular upset. The Soviet Union were favourites after qualifying top of their group, above European champions France. Nine of their starting line-up were drawn from the same team: the powerful Dynamo Kyiv. Igor Belanov's howitzer from outside the box put the Soviets 1–0 up at half-time, and he struck again following Enzo Scifo's leveller. A controversial equalizer by Jan Ceulemans (*right*) took the game to extra time, when Belgium took charge with two goals. Belanov completed his hat-trick from the spot but could not save the game.

15

26 Jun 1954

AUSTRIA 7
SWITZERLAND 5

Stade Olympique de la Pontaise, Lausanne, Switzerland

Austria	Switzerland
Wagner 25, 27, 53 A. Körner 26, 34 Ocwirk 32 Probst 76	Ballaman 16, 39 Hügi 17, 19, 60

This quarter-final from the 1954 tournament produced the **most goals in a FIFA World Cup match**, with the sides combining for 12. Two players – Austria's Theodor Wagner and Swiss striker Josef Hügi – scored hat-tricks. The amazing scoreline might have owed something to soaring temperatures of 40°C (104°F), which gave the game its nickname, "The Heated Battle of Lausanne". Switzerland were 3–0 up after 20 min but faded in the fierce sunshine. By half-time it was 5–4 to Austria, who also missed a penalty. There were three more goals in the second half but, surprisingly, none after the 76th min, as the punishing conditions took their toll on the players.

Brilliant Belanov

Following his heroic efforts in Mexico, Igor Belanov was awarded the 1986 Ballon d'Or, which was at that time open only to European footballers. The Soviet striker is one of three players – along with Ernst Wilimowski (1938) and Josef Hügi (1954, *see below*) – to score a World Cup hat-trick and lose the match. Cristiano Ronaldo (2018) and Kylian Mbappé (2022) are the only players to hit a treble and draw.

> "Everyone thought the Soviets would win easily. They had a great team and, what's more, they all played together."
>
> (Jean-Marie Pfaff)

FACT

The heat gave Austrian keeper Kurt Schmied sunstroke, but no substitutions were allowed and he chose to battle on, supported by team masseur Josef Ulrich (*right*). Afterwards, Schmied claimed to have no memory of playing in the game!

Most goals in a FIFA World Cup match

MATCH	YEAR	GOALS
Austria 7–5 Switzerland	1954	12
Brazil 6–5 Poland	1938	11
Hungary 8–3 West Germany	1954	11
Hungary 10–1 El Salvador	1982	11
France 7–3 Paraguay	1958	10

**France 4–6 England in 2026 also 10 goals*

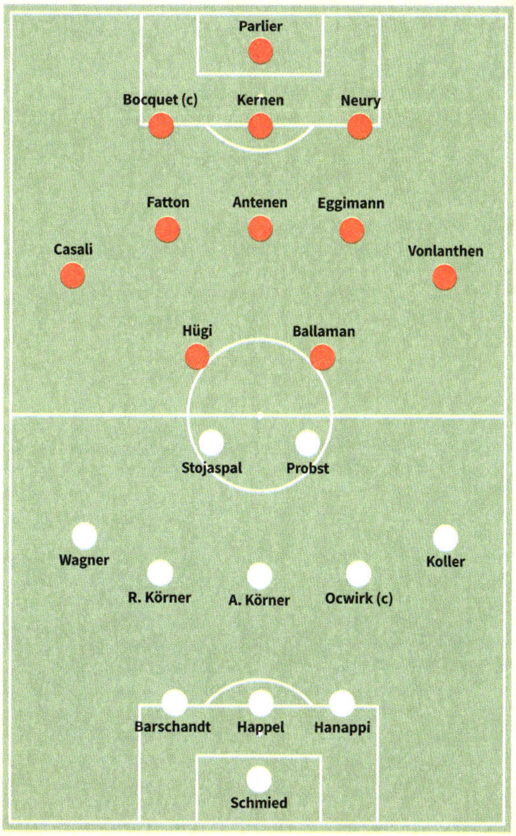

TEAM FORMATIONS

14

2 Jul 2010

URUGUAY 1–1 GHANA

Soccer City, Johannesburg, South Africa

Forlán 55 Muntari 45+2

Uruguay won 4–2 on penalties

"I made the save of the tournament."
(Luis Suárez)

The first-ever meeting between these two nations produced a classic, featuring perhaps the most infamous "save" in World Cup history. Ghana were aiming to become the first African side to reach the semi-finals and took the lead with a strike from Sulley Muntari. A wicked free-kick from Diego Forlán brought Uruguay level. In the dying seconds of extra time, the game erupted when a header from Dominic Adiyiah was palmed away on the line by Uruguay's Luis Suárez (*right*). The striker was sent off and Ghana's Asamoah Gyan had the chance to win the game from the spot – only to hit the crossbar. And it was Uruguay who held their nerve in the ensuing shootout, with Sebastián Abreu coolly sending a Panenka penalty past Richard Kingson.

13

23 Jul 1966

PORTUGAL 5
NORTH KOREA 3

Goodison Park, Liverpool, UK

Portugal	North Korea
Eusébio 27, 43 (pen.), 56, 59 (pen.)	Pak Seung-zin 1
Augusto 80	Li Dong-woon 22
	Yang Seung-kook 25

Despite their strong showing in 1966, North Korea have only played in one World Cup finals tournament since – in 2010, when their three defeats included a 7–0 thrashing by… Portugal.

This quarter-final match-up boasted one of the great World Cup comebacks. Underdogs North Korea had become unlikely fan favourites in England, shocking the football world by defeating Italy 1–0. They flew out of the traps against Portugal, Pak Seung-zin blasting home inside the first 60 sec. By 25 min, the North Koreans had raced into a 3–0 lead. Portugal star Eusébio began the fightback, scoring twice to reduce the deficit to one goal by half-time. He added two more in the second half, including a second spot-kick after he was fouled in the box. A fifth goal by José Augusto set the seal on Portugal's remarkable revival.

221
The **most games as head coach of an international football team** – by Uruguay manager Óscar Tabárez, between 1988 and 2021.

Paying the Penalty

Asamoah Gyan had previously missed a spot-kick at the 2006 World Cup, hitting the post against the Czech Republic. His second failure against Uruguay gave him the record for the **most FIFA World Cup penalties missed (excluding shootouts)**. This was equalled by Lionel Messi (ARG) in 2022 and then broken in 2026, when Messi missed two spot-kicks to take his career total to four.

TEAM FORMATIONS

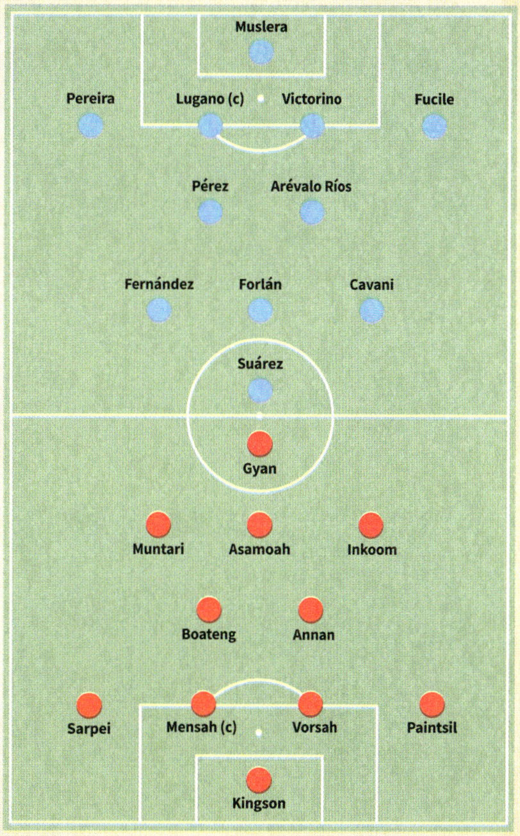

TEAM FORMATIONS

Eusébio finished the 1966 tournament as top scorer with nine goals.

Most penalties scored at the FIFA World Cup (excluding shootouts)

PLAYER	TEAM	GOALS	SUCCESS	YEAR(S)
Harry Kane	England	6	86%	2018–26
Eusébio	Portugal	4	100%	1966
Rob Rensenbrink	Netherlands	4	100%	1978
Gabriel Batistuta	Argentina	4	100%	1994–98
Cristiano Ronaldo	Portugal	4	80%	2006–26

**Lionel Messi (ARG) also on 4, with a 50% success rate*

12

18 Jun 2002

SOUTH KOREA 2–1 ITALY

Daejeon World Cup Stadium, South Korea

Seol Ki-hyeon 88 Ahn Jung-hwan 117	Vieri 18

Almost from the first whistle, controversy reigned in this dramatic Round-of-16 tie from 2002. Hosts South Korea were awarded a penalty minutes after kick-off, but Ahn Jung-hwan's effort was saved by Gianluigi Buffon. Italy took the lead through Christian Vieri (*inset*); a late equalizer sent the game into extra-time. Francesco Totti was shown a second yellow card for an alleged dive, and then Damiano Tommasi's goal was chalked off for offside. With Italy still crying foul, Ahn (*right*) rose highest to head home and seal a golden-goal victory for South Korea.

11

30 Jul 1966

ENGLAND 4
WEST GERMANY 2

Wembley Stadium, London, UK

Hurst 18, 101, 120 Peters 78	Haller 12 Weber 89

England and West Germany had only conceded three goals combined all tournament, but the 1966 final was an incident-packed thriller. Germany silenced the home fans by taking an early lead, only for strikes by Geoff Hurst and Martin Peters to put England on the verge of victory. A last-gasp equalizer from defender Wolfgang Weber took the game into extra time. The pivotal moment came in the 101st min, when Hurst's shot came down off the crossbar and was adjudged to have crossed the line by linesman Tofiq Bahramov. Hurst completed his hat-trick with the last kick of the game to send Wembley Stadium into raptures.

TEAM FORMATIONS

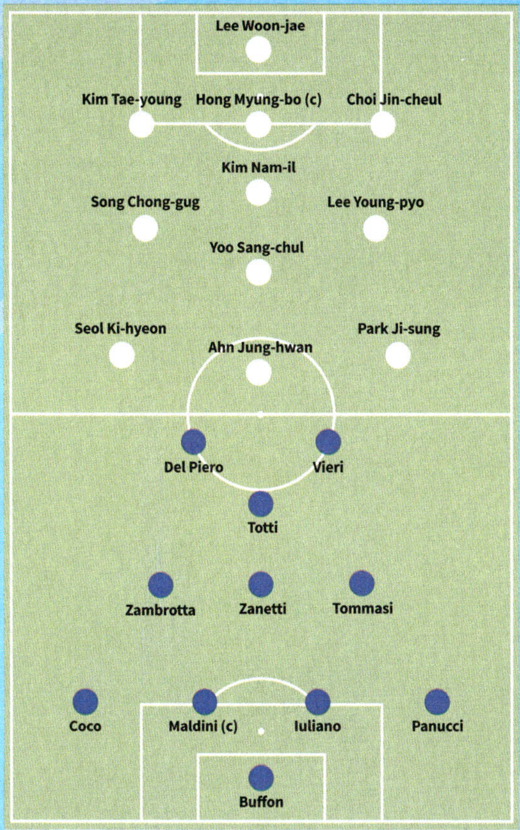

Asian Tigers

South Korea went on to become the first Asian team to reach the semi-finals of the FIFA World Cup. They defeated Spain in the quarter-finals on penalties – a game with its own moments of controversy, as Spain had two goals ruled out. In the semi-finals, South Korea finally fell to a narrow 1–0 loss to Germany.

FACT

South Korea hold the unenviable record for the **most goals conceded in a FIFA World Cup**. In 1954, they let in 16 goals in just two games!

FACT

England centre-back Bobby Moore set up Geoff Hurst's first and third goals, setting a record for the **most assists in a FIFA World Cup final**. Moore's feat would be equalled by Pelé for Brazil against Italy four years later.

Most goals in a FIFA World Cup final

Geoff Hurst struck three times for England against West Germany in 1966. He scored with his right foot, left foot and his head to record a perfect hat-trick. Hurst had only broken into the England line-up in the knockout phases of the tournament, following an injury to star striker Jimmy Greaves. His long-standing record was finally equalled by France's Kylian Mbappé in the 2022 final.

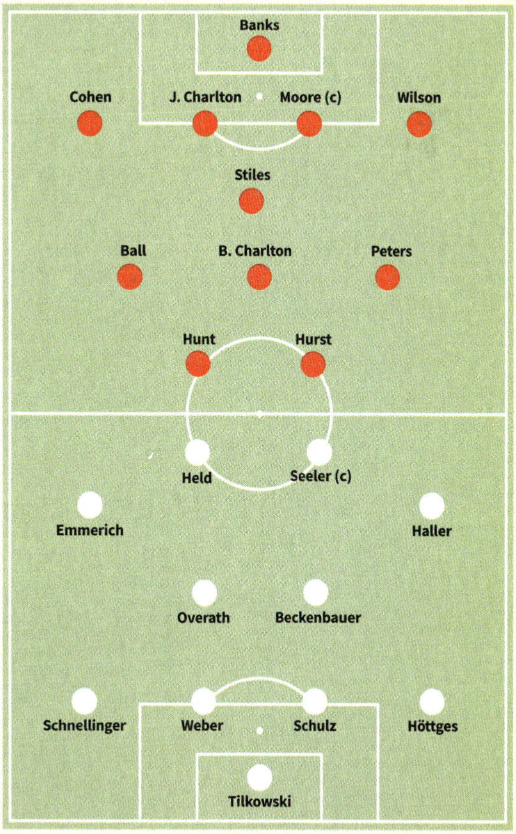

TEAM FORMATIONS

10

15 Jun 2018

PORTUGAL 3–3 SPAIN

Fisht Stadium, Sochi, Russia

Portugal	Spain
Ronaldo 4 (pen.), 44, 88	Costa 24, 55 Nacho 58

Iberian rivals Portugal and Spain served up a group-stage sizzler in 2018, sharing six goals between them. Inside the first five minutes, Cristiano Ronaldo won and converted a penalty (*right*) to register a goal at his fourth World Cup tournament. Diego Costa scored a bullish equalizer, only for Ronaldo to strike again, his shot going through Spanish keeper David de Gea. Costa equalized again in the second half before a spectacular half-volley from Nacho saw Spain take the lead for the first time. With the clock ticking down, Ronaldo stepped up to fire home a dipping free-kick from well outside the box, completing his hat-trick and earning a dramatic draw.

9

29 Jun 1958

BRAZIL 5
SWEDEN 2

Råsunda Stadium, Solna, Sweden

Brazil	Sweden
Vavá 9, 32 Pelé 55, 90 Zagallo 68	Liedholm 4 Simonsson 80

A two-time World Cup winner in 1958 and 1962, Brazil's Garrincha (above, right) bamboozled defenders with his explosive pace and outrageous dribbling skills.

With a total of seven goals, the **highest-scoring World Cup final** saw Brazil become the first side to lift the trophy on a foreign continent. The South Americans had to find a new second kit to wear after hosts Sweden won the right to wear yellow. The Europeans took an early lead, but a brace from Vavá put Brazil 2–1 up at the break. In the second half, wonderkid Pelé scored a magical third. Controlling the ball on his chest, he knocked it over the defender's head and volleyed it in. There followed a goal for either side before Pelé added Brazil's fifth with a header. At the final whistle he collapsed, overwhelmed by his country's first World Cup triumph.

Oldest player to score a hat-trick at the FIFA World Cup

Cristiano Ronaldo (b. 5 Feb 1985) was 33 years 130 days old when he scored three times for Portugal during their 3–3 draw with Spain on 15 Jun 2018. He surpassed the record of the Netherlands' Rob Rensenbrink, who hit a hat-trick against Iran at the 1978 World Cup at the age of 30 years 335 days. Lionel Messi (ARG, b. 24 Jun 1987) would eclipse both efforts in 2026, scoring three goals against Algeria aged 38 years 357 days.

Youngest scorer in a FIFA World Cup final

Pelé (b. 23 Oct 1940) was 17 years 249 days old when he scored a brace against Sweden. Injured at the start of the tournament, he didn't score until the knockout stages. Against Wales in the quarter-finals, Pelé became the **youngest World Cup goal scorer**, aged 17 years 239 days. He recorded a hat-trick against France in the semis, before his two-goal display in the final confirmed his status as the most exciting talent world football had ever seen.

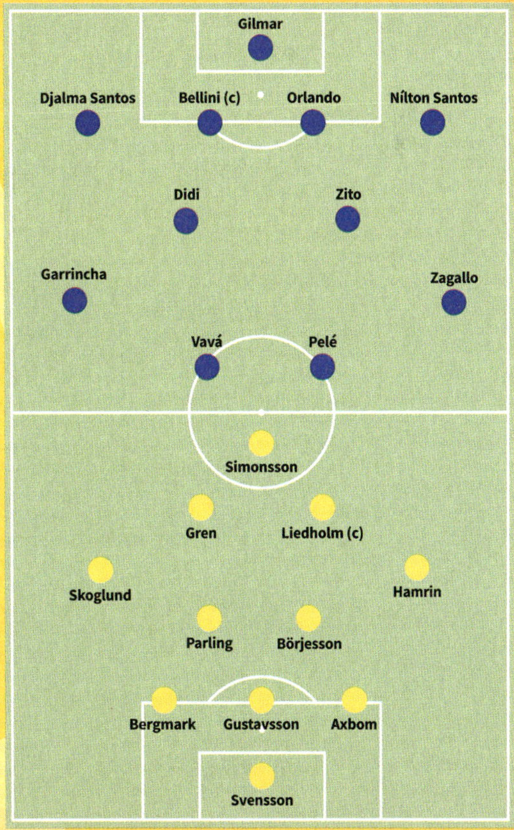

8

22 Jun 1986

ARGENTINA 2–1 ENGLAND

Estadio Azteca, Mexico City, Mexico

Maradona 51, 55 | Lineker 81

Perhaps more than any other World Cup match, this quarter-final from Mexico '86 will always be remembered for the actions of one player – Argentina's Diego Maradona. The first half ended goalless, but the game suddenly exploded into life when Maradona leapt with England goalkeeper Peter Shilton and punched the ball into the net with his fist (*right*). Over English protests, the goal was given. Minutes later, Maradona embarked on a dazzling run through the shellshocked defence, beating four outfield players and sliding the ball home. England pulled a goal back through the tournament's top scorer, Gary Lineker, but Argentina held on to secure an emotional – and controversial – victory.

7

30 Jun 1954

HUNGARY 4–2 URUGUAY

Stade Olympique de la Pontaise, Lausanne, Switzerland

Czibor 12
Hidegkuti 47
Kocsis 109, 116

Hohberg 75, 86

It was Uruguay's first defeat in the World Cup, but that Hungary team was really wonderful. (Juan Schiaffino)

Both sides had reason to be confident before this semi-final: Olympic champions Hungary were unbeaten in four years, while Uruguay had never lost a World Cup match. It was the Europeans who started the stronger, striking early and doubling their lead just after half-time with a diving header from Nándor Hidegkuti (*right*). But Uruguay rallied, and two late goals from forward Juan Hohberg sent the match into extra time. With the game in the balance, Hungary's Sándor Kocsis stepped up with a pair of headers to win an all-time classic.

FACT

Maradona's second goal against England was voted the FIFA World Cup Goal of the Century in an online poll taken in 2002. In second place was Michael Owen's 1998 effort for England... against Argentina.

Most expensive football shirt sold at auction

Maradona's no.10 shirt from the England quarter-final fetched £7,142,500 ($8.9 m) at Sotheby's in London on 4 May 2022. Argentina had played the tie in shirts bought only days before the game, having struggled in thicker cotton jerseys during their previous match against Uruguay. They sourced 38 shirts locally in Mexico City that were selected by Maradona himself. A designer sewed on the Argentine football federation badge and ironed on shirt numbers.

TEAM FORMATIONS

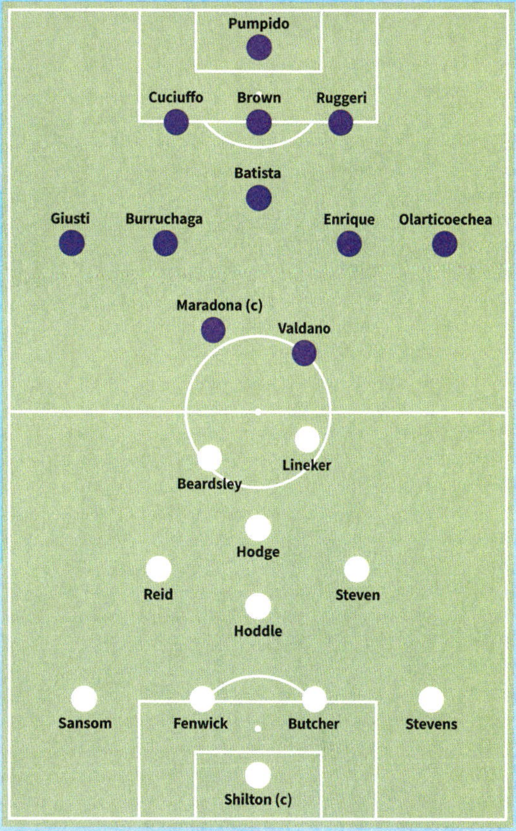

TEAM FORMATIONS

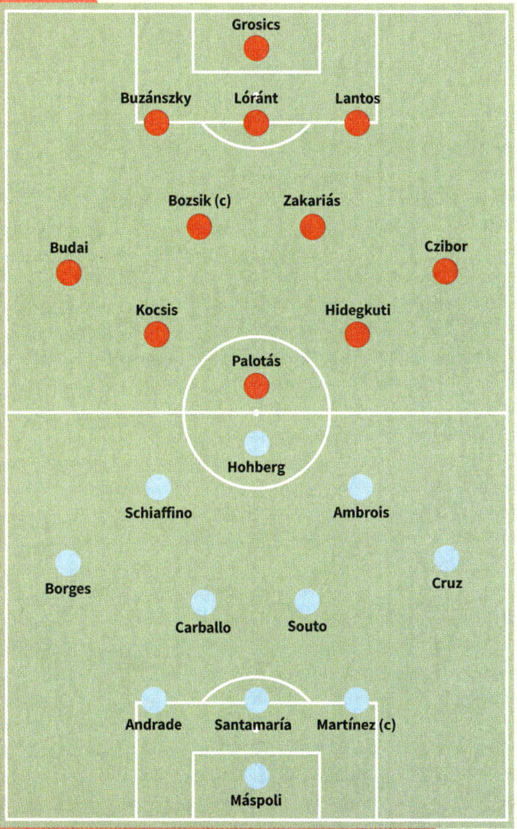

Most goals by a team at a FIFA World Cup tournament

Hungary netted 27 times in just five games in 1954 – an average of more than five per match. They were led by Sándor Kocsis, who hit a then-record 11 goals across the tournament. South Korea were humbled 9–0 in the group stages, and West Germany 8–3. But the Germans took their revenge in the final, coming from 2–0 down after just eight minutes to defeat Hungary 3–2 in a huge upset. The "Marvellous Magyars" remain arguably the greatest team never to lift the World Cup.

6

8 Jul 2014

BRAZIL 1–7 GERMANY

Estádio Mineirão, Belo Horizonte, Brazil

Brazil	Germany
Oscar 89	Müller 11 Klose 23 Kroos 24, 26 Khedira 29 Schürrle 69, 79

Not every classic is a close contest. The semi-final of the 2014 World Cup between Brazil and Germany produced one of the most memorable scorelines ever, and devastated an entire nation. Hosts Brazil went into the clash unbeaten but missing key players in Neymar and Thiago Silva. To the horror of the home fans (*inset*), Germany powered into a 5–0 lead within the first half hour, with man of the match Toni Kroos (*right*) netting twice. In the second half, sub André Schürrle scored two more as the Germans picked apart their shellshocked opponents. Oscar's late goal for Brazil was not even a consolation.

5

5 Jul 1982

ITALY 3
BRAZIL 2

Estadio Sarriá, Barcelona, Spain

Italy	Brazil
Rossi 5, 25, 74	Sócrates 12 Falcão 68

“The first goal against Brazil was the most important I ever scored... It gave me my confidence back completely.”
Paolo Rossi

This second group-stage match from 1982 was an epic clash of styles. Tournament favourites Brazil had wowed the crowds with their attacking play, whereas Italy were a well-drilled defensive unit. Italy coach Enzo Bearzot had been under pressure to drop misfiring striker Paolo Rossi, but his faith was rewarded as Rossi put Brazil to the sword. He scored his first with a darting header, only for Brazil to conjure an equalizer through their captain Sócrates. A defensive slip put Rossi through for his second; in the second half, a howitzer from Falcão brought the scores level again. But Rossi would not be denied, rifling home from a corner to seal a famous win.

Most FIFA World Cup final appearances by a team

Germany's astonishing win in Belo Horizonte booked their passage into a record eighth World Cup final. They went on to defeat Argentina 1–0 through a Mario Götze strike in extra time to lift the trophy for a fourth time. In the seven World Cup tournaments between 1966 and 1990, Germany (then West Germany) reached the final an incredible five times.

FACT

Germany's Miroslav Klose scored his 16th and final World Cup goal against Brazil. Five days later, after the final, he retired from international football having scored the **most FIFA World Cup goals**. This record was beaten by Lionel Messi and Kylian Mbappé in 2026 – *see pp.122–123*.

TEAM FORMATIONS

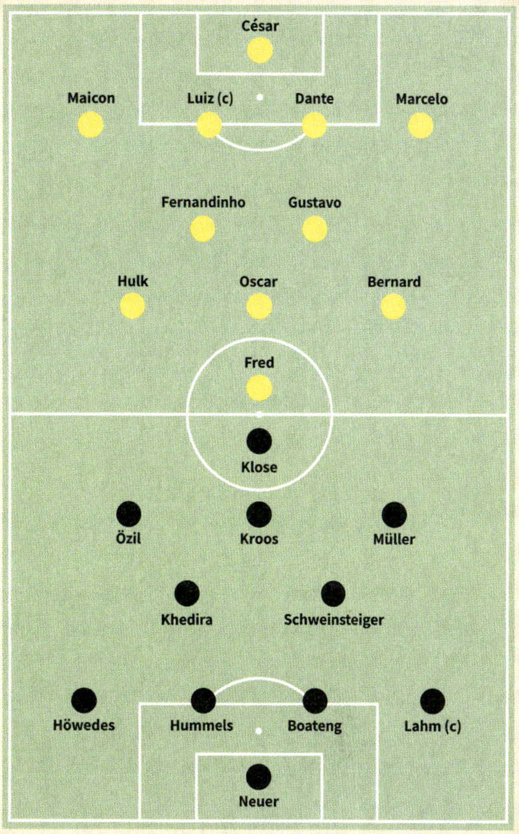

TEAM FORMATIONS

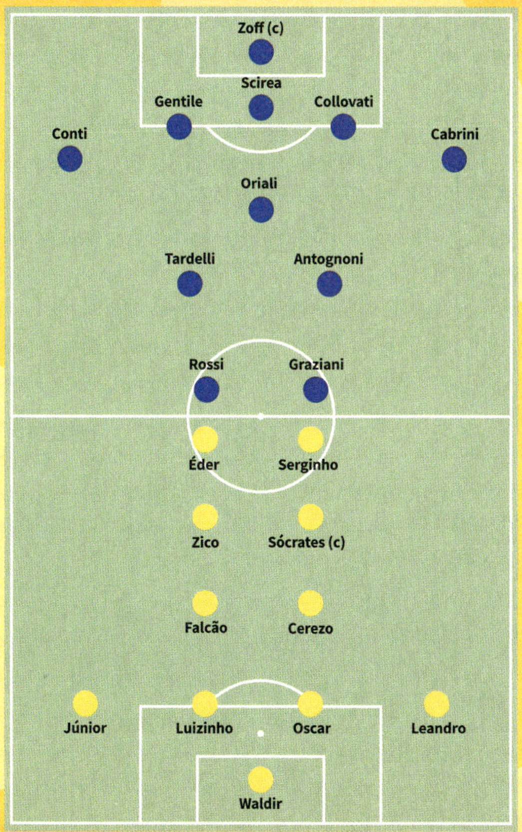

King of Keepers

Italy goalkeeper Dino Zoff made a vital save in the final seconds of the game against Brazil, just keeping an Oscar header from crossing the line. Italy went on to defeat Poland and West Germany to lift the trophy, making Zoff (b. 28 Feb 1942) the **oldest FIFA World Cup winner** at the age of 40 years 133 days. The veteran stopper had made his international debut 14 years earlier at the 1968 UEFA European Championship, which Italy also won.

4

17 Jun 1970

ITALY 4–3 WEST GERMANY

Estadio Azteca, Mexico City, Mexico

Boninsegna 8	Schnellinger 90+2
Burgnich 98	Müller 94, 110
Riva 104	
Rivera 111	

This heavyweight clash in the semi-final of the 1970 World Cup became known as the "Game of the Century", and featured five goals in extra time. Italy led for most of normal time following Roberto Boninsegna's early strike. Things got worse for West Germany in the second half, as their midfield linchpin Franz Beckenbauer suffered a dislocated shoulder. Bravely, "Der Kaiser" opted to play on. A last-gasp equalizer meant extra time. The two sides traded goals, both taking the lead. After a Gerd Müller header had made it 3–3, Italy regrouped and scored within a minute, sub Gianni Rivera sidefooting home to spark jubilant scenes back in Italy.

"No one has forgotten that match. I haven't recovered from it to this day." (Gerd Müller)

3

18 Dec 2022

ARGENTINA 3
FRANCE 3

Lusail Stadium, Lusail, Qatar

Messi 23 (pen.), 108	Mbappé 80 (pen.),
Di María 36	81, 118 (pen.)

Argentina won 4–2 on penalties

Lionel Messi's two goals in the final took his total at Qatar 2022 to seven – the ***most goals by a captain in a FIFA World Cup tournament****. This record was broken in 2026 by France's Kylian Mbappé, who netted 10 times.*

The 2022 World Cup was decided in the most dramatic way imaginable, as Argentina triumphed on penalties following a breathless 3–3 draw with France. The South Americans raced into a 2–0 lead through a Messi penalty and a lightning-quick counter-attack by Ángel Di María. Deep into the second half, Kylian Mbappé led a French fightback, scoring twice in as many minutes. Messi struck again in extra time, only for Mbappé to put away his second spot-kick. He converted a third in the shootout, but misses from Coman and Tchouaméni saw Argentina prevail 4–2.

TEAM FORMATIONS

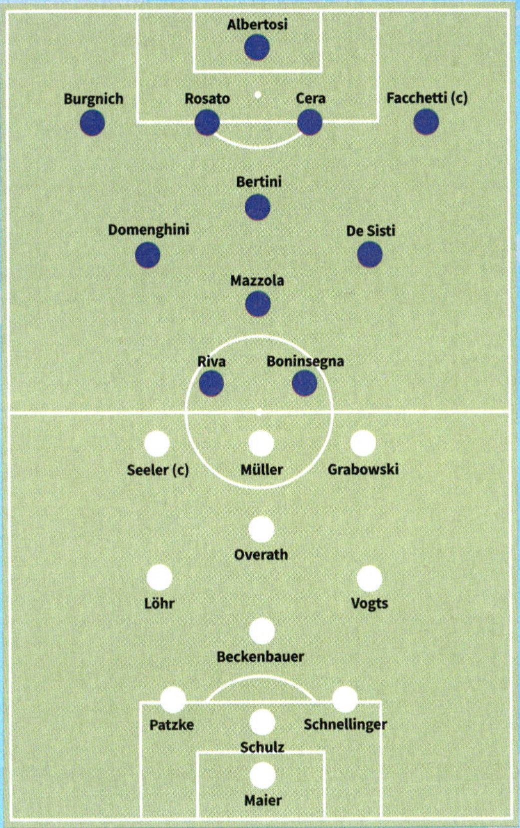

PLAYER PROFILE

Gerd Müller

Müller's brace against Italy took his tournament total in 1970 to 10, earning him the Golden Boot. A voracious goal-hunter nicknamed "Der Bomber", Müller retired from international football after scoring the winner in the 1974 World Cup final. His record for West Germany stands at 68 goals in just 62 games. Müller's total of 14 World Cup goals was the all-time record for 32 years, until Brazil's Ronaldo reached 15 in 2006.

FACT

West Germany's injury-time equalizer came from an unlikely source – defender Karl-Heinz Schnellinger, who was playing his club football in Italy for AC Milan at the time. It was the only international goal Schnellinger scored.

Most FIFA World Cup final goals by a player

Kylian Mbappé's hat-trick against Argentina took his tally of goals in World Cup finals to four. He had also scored during France's 4–2 win over Croatia in 2018, becoming only the second teenager after Pelé to score in the showpiece match. As of 2022, Mbappé stood one final goal ahead of Pelé, Vavá, Zinedine Zidane and Geoff Hurst (*see p.145*).

TEAM FORMATIONS

2

8 Jul 1982

WEST GERMANY 3–3 FRANCE

Ramón Sánchez Pizjuán Stadium, Seville, Spain

West Germany	France
Littbarski 17	Platini 27 (pen.)
Rummenigge 102	Trésor 92
Fischer 108	Giresse 98

West Germany won 5–4 on penalties

Two European heavyweights went toe-to-toe in an electrifying semi-final settled by the **first FIFA World Cup penalty shootout**. The score was 1–1 when the game's key moment occurred: German keeper Toni Schumacher escaping punishment after knocking sub Patrick Battiston unconscious in a challenge (*inset*). France rallied to race into a 3–1 lead in extra time, thanks to strikes from Trésor and Giresse. But West Germany roared back, Klaus Fischer levelling the scores with a bicycle kick (*right*). In the penalty shootout, Schumacher turned from villain to hero, saving two spot-kicks to seal the win.

1

21 Jun 1970

BRAZIL 4
ITALY 1

Estadio Azteca, Mexico City, Mexico

Brazil	Italy
Pelé 18	Boninsegna 37
Gérson 66	
Jairzinho 71	
Carlos Alberto 86	

Jairzinho scored in all of Brazil's games in 1970, including the final – the only player to do so in the history of the FIFA World Cup.

Both Brazil and Italy lined up for the 1970 final seeking an unprecedented third World Cup win – but it was the South Americans who made history, with a performance filled with creativity and attacking flair. They took the lead through a Pelé header, only for a defensive lapse to let in Italy's Roberto Boninsegna for an equalizer. In the second half, a thunderbolt from Gérson pierced the Italians' dogged defence before Jairzinho bundled home. To round off the win, captain Carlos Alberto scored one of the World Cup's most famous goals, smashing home after a flowing team move. As three-time winners, Brazil were allowed to keep the Jules Rimet Trophy.

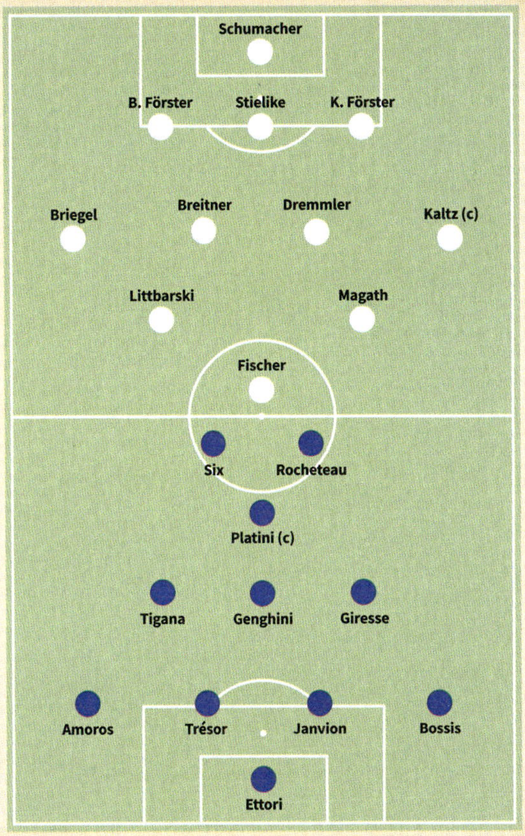

Longest penalty shootout at the FIFA World Cup

West Germany and France took a combined total of 12 spot-kicks in their 1982 semi-final shootout. Both sides missed one before French right-back Maxime Bossis saw his penalty saved, allowing sub Horst Hrubesch the opportunity to convert the winner. This record was equalled by Romania and Sweden in 1994 (Sweden won 5–4) and by Germany and Paraguay in 2026 (Paraguay won 4–3).

> "That was my most beautiful game. It was complete. It was fabulous."
> (Michel Platini)

Most wins of the FIFA World Cup by a player

Pelé received three winners' medals following Brazil's triumphs in 1958, 1962 and 1970. He played in four tournaments in total, becoming the first player to score in three consecutively in 1966. Although Pelé's tournament in 1962 was cut short by injury, he was retrospectively awarded a medal by FIFA in 2007. His 1970 winner's medal fetched £346,000 ($498,994) at auction in 2016 – making it the **most expensive football medal**.

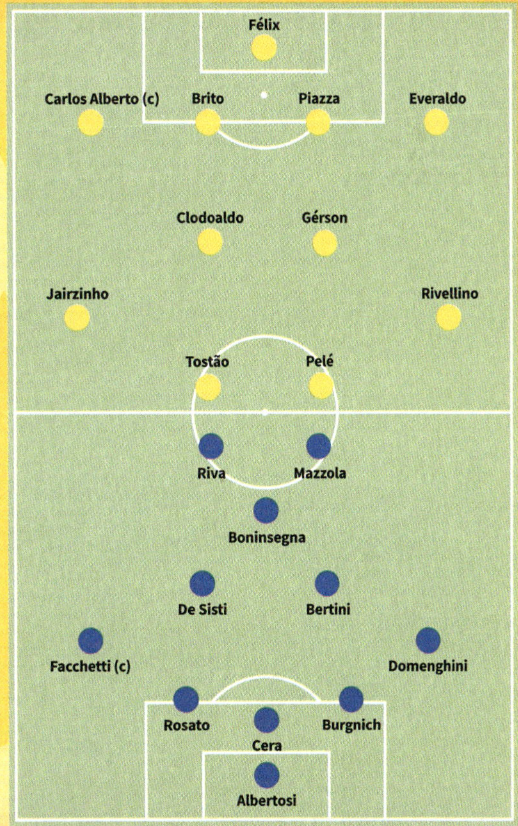

TEAM FORMATIONS

SCANDALS & SHOCKERS

Not every match can be a classic, even at the World Cup. From bitter brawls to no-score bores, these games hit the headlines for all the wrong reasons...

1962

CHILE 2–0 ITALY

The "Battle of Santiago" was so violent that the police had to enter the pitch four times to stop the players fighting.

Tensions between the two sides had been stoked in the newspapers leading up to the match, and it took only minutes for Italy's Giorgio Ferrini to be sent off – he refused to leave and was removed by a policeman. His teammate Mario David was also red-carded before half-time, and the scuffles continued to the final whistle.

1938

BRAZIL 1
CZECHOSLOVAKIA 1

One of the most brutal games in the history of international football, the "Battle of Bordeaux" saw three red cards issued and players from both sides suffer severe injuries.

Czech striker Oldřich Nejedlý left the field with a broken leg, while keeper František Plánička played on with a broken arm and had to retire from football afterwards. The replay (*above*) saw Brazil win 2–1, with both teams fielding much-changed line-ups.

1982

HUNGARY 10
EL SALVADOR 1

This one-sided encounter remains the only time a team has reached double digits at the FIFA World Cup.

El Salvador had fallen into civil war, the squad had been cut by its own federation, and the team adopted a risky attacking strategy for the Hungary match. The score was only 3–0 at half-time, but in the second half the floodgates opened. Substitute László Kiss registered the **fastest FIFA World Cup hat-trick**, scoring three in just 7 min. He also had another ruled out for offside. At least El Salvador could celebrate their first – and, to date, only – World Cup goal, courtesy of Luis Ramírez Zapata.

2006

SWITZERLAND 0–0 UKRAINE

Widely criticised as one of the dullest games in World Cup history, this knockout tie offered almost nothing in the way of drama. After 120 min of scrappy, cautious play in Cologne, Germany, Switzerland missed all three of their spot-kicks to lose the shootout and exit the competition – remarkably, becoming the first team to do so without conceding a single goal all tournament.

1978

BRAZIL 1
SWEDEN 1

An engrossing group game became infamous for its final few moments. As the clock ticked past 90 min with the game all square at 1–1, a Brazilian corner was headed in by Zico.

But South American celebrations were cut short when referee Clive Thomas ruled it out, having blown his whistle for full-time just 6 sec into injury time, with the ball still in the air. Thomas himself later described his call as "probably the most controversial decision that any referee has ever made".

1982

WEST GERMANY 1
AUSTRIA 0

The final game of Group 2 at the 1982 World Cup was dubbed the "Disgrace of Gijón".

With rivals Algeria having already played their last game, both sides knew that a narrow win for West Germany would see both themselves and Austria progress. After an early German goal, both teams made little attempt to score, to the annoyance of the watching crowd. Following the tournament, FIFA changed the rules to ensure that all final group games kicked off at the same time.

2006

PORTUGAL 1–0 NETHERLANDS

This tetchy and ill-disciplined Round-of-16 clash saw referee Valentin Ivanov give out 16 bookings and produce the **most red cards in a FIFA World Cup game** – four. Dutch midfielder Mark van Bommel saw yellow after just 2 min, with his teammate Khalid Boulahrouz following suit shortly afterwards for a foul that forced off Cristiano Ronaldo. Portugal won the "Battle of Nuremberg" 1–0, but in terms of red cards it was a 2–2 draw: Boulahrouz and Giovanni van Bronckhorst were sent off for the Netherlands, and Costinha and Deco for Portugal.

EXTRA TIME

The ref might have blown his whistle for full time, but there's still lots of fun to be had. Meet the freestylers keen to show off their skills, put your football knowledge to the test, and see if you've got what it takes to earn your very own GWR record title...

CONTENTS

LARGEST FOOTBALL LESSON

On 15 Mar 2026, Mexico City's iconic Zócalo plaza was filled with 8,873 football fans keen to hone their skills in preparation for the FIFA World Cup. Under the watchful eye of coaches and former Mexican internationals such as Óscar Pérez and Francisco Fonseca, the soccer students practised for around 40 min, dressed in the green, white and red colours of the Mexican flag. They beat the previous record of 1,038 people, set in 2025 in Seattle, USA.

Another record to fall as part of Mexico's World Cup build-up was the **largest human image of a shirt** (*above*). A total of 4,757 people arranged themselves into an *El Tri* national football top at Estadio Víctor Manuel Reyna in Tuxtla Gutiérrez on 27 Feb 2026.

WORLD OF FREESTYLE

Mixing juggling, ball control and acrobatics, freestyle is the ultimate fusion of creativity and technique – with a dash of street style thrown in. This rapidly growing sport has reached all parts of the globe, as you can see from the latest feats of our record-breaking community...

1

VENEZUELA: LAURA BIONDO

The first Latin American freestyle world champion, Laura has also performed with Cirque du Soleil. On 2 Sep 2025, she visited GWR HQ in London and performed the **most women's clipper tricks in one minute** – 48 – to reclaim a title she last held in 2017. Laura also completed the **most women's around the moon tricks in 30 seconds** – 27.

3

FRANCE: MÉLODY DONCHET

Mélody took up freestyle when injury derailed her chances of becoming a professional footballer, and went on to win six world championships. On 26 Jan 2026, she hung tough to achieve her latest world record: the **most consecutive football touches while hanging with one hand in 30 seconds** – 100.

2

SWEDEN: DANIEL YAAKOB

On 30–31 May 2025, TikTok freestyler Daniel took on one of GWR's most iconic freestyle record titles: the **longest time doing keep-ups.** He juggled a ball for 28 hr 21 min 2 sec at the Rydshallen sports complex in Linköping, Sweden. Daniel kicked off his marathon at 4 a.m., banking five minutes of rest every hour. He rounded off his Herculean effort with one last around the world trick.

IRAN: MARYAM NIKBAKHT

On 19 Oct 2025, Iranian freestyler Maryam completed the **most women's keep-ups with the shin in one minute** – 228 – in Tehran, Iran. That's almost four every second! She smashed the previous record by 77 touches.

UAE: HAMED ALI ALSHEHHI

Hamed is the holder of multiple football world records. On 21 Aug 2025, he ran the **fastest 1 km juggling a football**, going the distance in 7 min 13 sec in Ras Al Khaimah, UAE. Hamed also went on to achieve the **fastest time to hit both goalposts and crossbar** – 6.57 sec, from the 18-yard line – on 17 Dec 2025.

CHINA: QI TAO

Qi Tao fell in love with football at the age of 16 – four years later, he was ready to take on a world record. On 30 Jun 2025 in Kunming, China, Tao completed the **most keep-ups with one foot in one hour** – a staggering 12,086, or around 200 every minute! He spent six months in intensive training before making his attempt.

JAPAN: JUNYA HITOMI

Freestyler Junya, aka HITO, is the master of the slap trick – a flick performed by rolling the ball up the outside of the calf with the toe of the opposite foot. On 20 Feb 2025, he achieved the **most slap tricks in one minute** – 81 – in Kyoto, Japan. Later that year, Junya executed the **most consecutive slap tricks** – 191.

STEP BROTHERS

Between them, brothers James and Ben Taylor (both UK) have earned an impressive seven GWR freestyle titles. Their tricks and flicks have taken them on an incredible journey that's seen them perform at competitions and on matchdays before thousands of football fans. On 11 Apr 2026, James achieved the **most around-the-world tricks in one minute (under 16s)** – 76 – at half-time during Cardiff City's EFL League One match against Bolton Wanderers. We caught up with the skilful siblings to find out more.

Touchline chat in between performances at EFL Championship side Swansea City.

Ben stepped up when we threw down the freestyle gauntlet in last year's *GWR Football Edition*, challenging our readers to complete a brand-new record title: the **fastest time to complete three FREESTYLE 5 tricks (under 16s)**. Ben's time of 6.3 sec earned him not only the under-16 record, but the overall title too! He's set to follow older brother James on the path to freestyle glory.

How old were you when you started freestyling?
I learned my first freestyle skill, the around the world, when I was nine. Once I was able to do that, I started doing more skills and just really enjoyed it.

What made you decide to take on our freestyle challenge?
I was really excited when I saw it in the *GWR Football Edition*, especially as I'd met Isabel [*Wilkins, who performed the how-to guide*] and know that she's an amazing freestyler.

Did seeing James break world records act as an inspiration?
It was really fun to see my brother breaking records and I wanted to be able to do that too! James has shown me that if you practise something enough you can get better and better, sometimes even good enough to break a world record.

How much time did you spend training for your attempt?
I had already been practising the individual moves that make up the FREESTYLE 5, so then I started putting them together in the right sequence. The more I did it the faster I got, which was really fun.

How did it feel when you found out you had earned a GWR title?
I was so excited! I don't think my friends believed me at first, so I had to take my certificate into school so that I could prove it to them all. It was really funny to see their reactions.

Ben blitzed our FREESTYLE 5 challenge in just 6.3 sec – and without wearing shoes!

With GWR Adjudicator Glenn Pollard at Cardiff City Stadium, after another successful record attempt.

A rising star of freestyle, James Taylor holds five GWR titles, including the **most consecutive alternating rebounder volleys** – 6,023 – and the **most shoulder rolls in 30 seconds** – 41 (*pictured below*).

What made you take up freestyling?
I really like the creativity and being able to experiment with new ideas and movements.

How often do you practise?
Every day. I really like practising, especially when you can see improvements or land a skill that you've been working on for a long time.

Who are your freestyle inspirations?
The Fagerli brothers (Erlend and Brynjar), Jesse Marlet and Tristan Gac. They are all so creative and inspiring – but also just really nice people!

What made you decide to try and break a world record?
My favourite skill when I was younger was the shoulder roll. I realized there was a world record for it, which was actually set in the year that I was born!

Which record was the hardest to achieve?
I found the **most hotstepper tricks in one minute** [95] the most difficult. Although the skill looks quite easy, it's really hard to get the rhythm right and it's also very tiring!

How did it feel when Ben set a world record of his own?
I was so pleased for him and so proud of him. We've made a pact that we won't try to break each other's world records!

What's your advice for freestylers who want to hone their skills?
Try to master the basic skills first, like kicky-ups and around the worlds. There are loads of online tutorials to help you. Mostly, though, enjoy it!

James regularly competes at freestyle events across Europe, and has won titles in Italy and the Netherlands.

The rebounder volley record was tough to beat, but James played for an hour to smash the previous total.

James

Taking centre stage with the Wales Under-21 squad.

YOU vs GWR

Once again, we've thrown down the gauntlet to our readers – with an even tougher test than before! Freestyle ace Isabel Wilkins is back to walk you through the steps. Have you got what it takes to complete the **fastest FREESTYLE 7 football trick (under 16s)**?

TRIPLE CROWN

Isabel Wilkins (UK, b. 29 Aug 2007) turned to freestyle during the COVID-19 lockdown, honing her skills in the back garden. Her first pro tournament was the 2023 Super Ball World Open, which she won aged 15 years 347 days to become the **youngest freestyle football world champion**. Isabel defended her crown the following year, and in Dec 2025 her third global title followed at the World Freestyle Football Championship in Sopot, Poland. Isabel's freestyle skills have earned her multiple GWR titles. She earned four in a single day on 8 Jan 2024, including the **most women's hop-the-world tricks in 30 seconds** – 47.

1

Begin with the ball on the ground. Use your knee to roll it forward in the direction of your feet as you move into a seated position.

2

Control the rolling ball between both of your feet. Toss the ball up into the air and catch it between your knees.

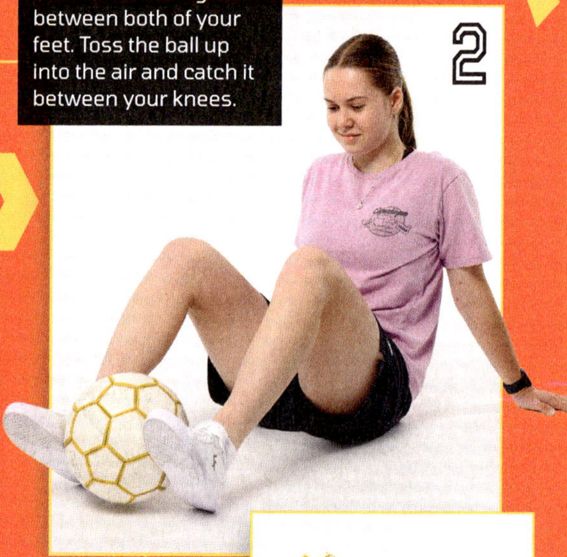

If you want to see Isabel perform the FREESTYLE 7 in full, scan the QR code to find a video of her in action!

3

With the ball secured between your knees, place your weight on one hand and begin to rotate yourself into a standing position.

4

Make sure that you don't drop the ball as you stand up - or it's attempt over!

5

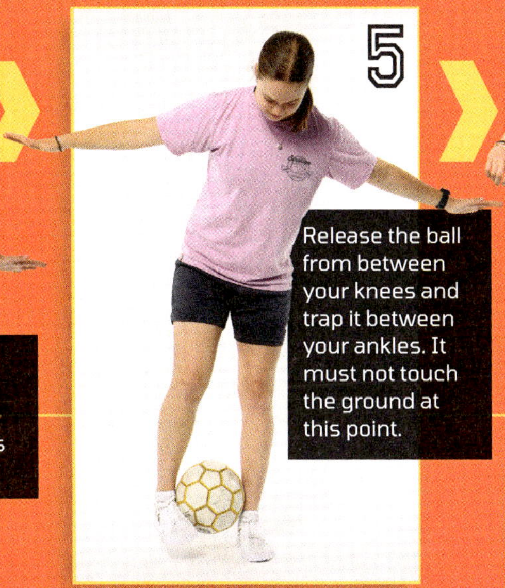

Release the ball from between your knees and trap it between your ankles. It must not touch the ground at this point.

6

You're almost there but there's still work to do. Flick the ball with your heels into the air.

7

While the ball is in the air, rearrange your feet so you can do a single keep-up. It doesn't matter which foot you use.

8

Catch the ball in your hands to end the FREESTYLE 7! How quick was your time? Can you do it faster?

How to apply

So you've been smashing it out of the park in training, and think you've got what it takes to become a freestyle world record holder. Before you begin your record attempt, go to our website – **guinnessworldrecords.com** – and register for an account. Read the record guidelines carefully so that you make sure you've got everything you need. Once you're happy with your attempt, you'll need to send us all the evidence - this will include videos, photos and witness statements. This record is part of our under-16s category, so we'll also need proof of your age. Adults need not apply! If you're successful, we'll send you an email confirmation a few weeks later. You can pick up your certificate from the GWR Store, showing that you are now a member of the GWR family – just like Isabel!

EXTRA TIME

FOOTBALL FUN

Football might be a serious business, but here we pay tribute to the lighter side of the game. Whether it's getting creative with soccer balls or using shirts to earn GWR glory, these are the kind of records that everyone can be part of!

MIND MASTER

On 8 Jun 2026, memory athlete Fabian Saal (DEU) came to London's GWR HQ to amaze our *What's the Record?* podcast with his powers of recall... and ball control! Fabian set four records, including the **most FIFA World Cup match results memorized while...**

- **doing keep-ups in 30 seconds** – five
- **juggling three objects in one minute** – 19 (*above*).

LARGEST COLLECTION OF FOOTBALL SHIRTS

Gustavo Arbelaez (COL) owns a treasure trove of 8,538 jerseys in Medellín, Colombia. He began collecting in 2005, during a trip to Brazil to watch his beloved Independiente Medellín take on Club Paranaense. Arbelaez bought a Grêmio shirt, kick-starting his love affair with football tops.

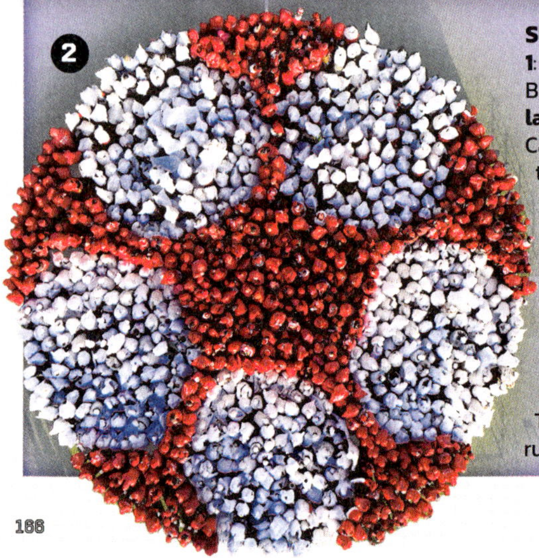

SUPERSIZED SOCCER CREATIONS

1: On 6 Sep 2025, Angel City FC and PNC Bank (both USA) teamed up to spell out the **largest football sentence** using 1,461 soccer balls in Los Angeles, California, USA. The resulting message – "RISE UP L.A." – paid tribute to the city's response to the devastating wildfires that had swept through the region earlier that year.

2: The **largest human image of a football**, made up of 1,198 people, was created on 27 Dec 2025 in Saitama, Japan. It was assembled at Redsland, a sports facility owned by J1 League outfit Urawa Red Diamonds.

3: On 11 Apr 2026, the **longest line of footballs** – 1,036 balls – was laid out by soccer fans including ex-USA international DaMarcus Beasley and rapper Bun B in Houston, Texas, USA. The event was arranged by Airbnb (USA) to celebrate the run-up to the FIFA World Cup.

LONGEST SEQUENTIAL FOOTBALL JUGGLE RELAY

On 6 Jun 2026, German youth footballers from the Altona 93 boys and HSV girls teams took up an unusual skills challenge on an S-Bahn train in Hamburg. Participants took turns to do keep-ups, with each new person taking one more touch than the last. Both the boys and the girls teams reached 15 players without breaking the chain. The carriage was even laid with grass to make the footballers feel at home!

MOST NATIONALITIES PASSING A FOOTBALL

On 17 Sep 2025, UEFA Champions League sponsor Mastercard brought together representatives from 50 countries to pass the ball along Saudi Arabia's Highway 10. Participating nations included Saint Kitts and Nevis, Eritrea and Kyrgyzstan.

MOST PROFESSIONAL FOOTBALL SHIRTS WORN AT ONCE

On 28 Apr 2026, football influencer and TikTok star Tom McGowan (NZ) paid a visit to GWR HQ in London in an attempt to bag his first world record title. He squeezed on a total of 40 soccer tops – including the famous blue-and-white stripes of Argentina – to become the inaugural holder.

HIGHEST-ALTITUDE FOOTBALL DROPPED AND CONTROLLED

On 23 Sep 2025, a ball dropped 40.08 m (131 ft 5 in) was brought under control by freestyler Philip Warren Gertsson (NOR/PHL). He juggled the ball five times without it touching the ground to qualify for the record. Gertsson beat the record of 38.92 m (127 ft 8 in), by ex-England international Jamie Redknapp. The attempt was staged by adidas to celebrate the release of the Trionda, the official match ball for the 2026 FIFA World Cup.

QUIZ

Put your footballing expertise to the test by tackling our 15 fiendish questions. How many can you get right? If you get stumped, you'll find helpful clues scattered throughout the book – and the answers are on p.175.

1 In which country would you find the Swamp Soccer World Championships?
- A USA
- B Bangladesh
- C Finland

2 Olivia Smith became the first women's £1-m player in 2025, when she moved from Liverpool to Arsenal. Which country does she play for?
- A England
- B Canada
- C USA

3 Which of these players broke the world transfer record twice?
- A Diego Maradona
- B Zinedine Zidane
- C Neymar

4 Which international men's side are known as the Lions of Teranga?
- A Ghana
- B Côte d'Ivoire
- C Senegal

5 Which Real Madrid player scored from his own half in a La Liga game against Elche in 2026?
- A Federico Valverde
- B Arda Güler
- C Trent Alexander-Arnold

6 How many countries have won the UEFA European Championships?
- A 6
- B 8
- C 10

7 Spanish teams have won the European Cup/UEFA Champions League a record 20 times. Which country is next on the list, with 15 wins?
- A Germany
- B Italy
- C England

8 Who is the only player to win the Kopa Trophy for the world's best under-21 player twice?
- A Kylian Mbappé
- B Lamine Yamal
- C Jude Bellingham

9 The longest penalty shootout at the FIFA Women's World Cup consisted of 20 spot-kicks. Which two teams were involved?

- **A** Australia and France
- **B** Colombia and Spain
- **C** USA and Netherlands

10 Nigeria have won 10 of the 13 Women's Africa Cup of Nations tournaments to date. Which other two countries have also lifted the trophy?

- **A** Equatorial Guinea and South Africa
- **B** Morocco and Zambia
- **C** Ghana and Cameroon

11 Brazilian striker Leônidas is often credited with inventing which flashy football move in the 1930s?

- **A** Step over
- **B** Rabona
- **C** Bicycle kick

12 Manchester City star Khadija Shaw has hit the most WSL hat-tricks – eight. Half of them have come against which side?

- **A** Everton
- **B** Tottenham Hotspur
- **C** Brighton

13 Which club in Japan's J1 League claimed a record ninth title in 2025?

- **A** Kashima Antlers
- **B** Kawasaki Frontale
- **C** Gamba Osaka

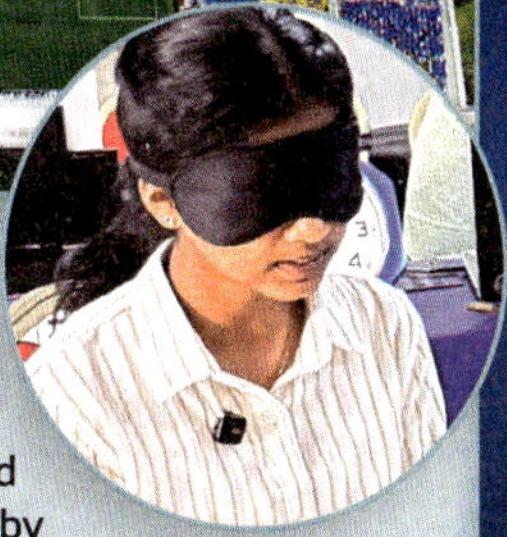

MOST FOOTBALL STADIUMS IDENTIFIED IN ONE MINUTE

On 14 Dec 2025, Elaina Terese from India correctly named the grounds belonging to 47 randomly generated clubs. She beat the previous record by 14. The stadiums were located around the world, and ranged from Cagliari's Unipol Domus in Italy to La Bombonera (*above*), home of Argentina's Boca Juniors.

14 In 2026, James Milner set a new EPL appearance record when he played in his 645th league match. He made his debut 23 seasons earlier for which team?

- **A** Newcastle United
- **B** Sunderland
- **C** Leeds United

15 Which is the only team to date to score 10 goals in a FIFA World Cup match?

- **A** Denmark
- **B** Hungary
- **C** France

Bold entries in the index indicate a player in the GWR Class of '27.

ACKNOWLEDGEMENTS

Alex Rowen, Chelsea FC (Sam Few & Charlie Long), CMG Sports (Bradley Rains), Daniel Cutting, FAM Sports (Jake Galbraith), Fem11 (Antje Blumhagen & Jörg Neblung), Getty Images (Chefik Simo & Richard Pitts), Isabel & Kate Wilkins, LAFC (Danny Sanchez), Lobeco GmbH (André Wersching), Paris Saint-Germain Football Club (Julien Maynard), Status Creative/CR88 Sports (Connor Rice), U.S. Soccer Federation (Nick Burton & Maria Howell), Zlatko Dalić

PICTURE CREDITS

Cover UK/Brazil/France/Sweden/Norway Christina Pahnke – sampics/Corbis via Getty Images, Shaun Brooks – CameraSport via Getty Images, Robbie Jay Barratt – AMA/Getty Images, Lars Baron/Getty Images, Eddie Keogh/Getty Images; **Cover USA** Omar Vega/Getty Images, Shaun Brooks – CameraSport via Getty Images, Robbie Jay Barratt – AMA/Getty Images, Lars Baron/Getty Images, Shaun Clark/ISI Photos/USSF/Getty Images; **Cover Croatia** Christina Pahnke – sampics/Corbis via Getty Images, Shaun Brooks – CameraSport via Getty Images, Joe Prior/Visionhaus via Getty Images, Lars Baron/Getty Images, Eddie Keogh/Getty Images; **Cover Spain** Christina Pahnke – sampics/Corbis via Getty Images, Shaun Brooks – CameraSport via Getty Images, Koji Watanabe/Getty Images, Lars Baron/Getty Images, Eddie Keogh/Getty Images; **Cover Germany** Christina Pahnke – sampics/Corbis via Getty Images, Shaun Brooks – CameraSport via Getty Images, Robbie Jay Barratt – AMA/Getty Images, Lars Baron/Getty Images, Dean Mouhtaropoulos/Getty Images; **Cover Italy** Robbie Jay Barratt – AMA/Getty Images, Shaun Brooks – CameraSport via Getty Images, Koji Watanabe/Getty Images, Lars Baron/Getty Images, Joe Prior/Visionhaus via Getty Images; **1** Jose Jacome/EPA/Shutterstock, Cory Knowlton/ZUMA Press Wire/Shutterstock, Oscar Manuel Sanchez/ZUMA Press Wire/Shutterstock, Justin Setterfield/Getty Images, Alex Grimm – FIFA/FIFA via Getty Images; **6** Lexy Ilsley/Manchester City FC, Masakazu Senda/GWR, Craig Foy/SNS Group/Celtic FC, Fourleaflover/Shutterstock, Justin Setterfield/Getty Images; **7** John Gillooly/PEI, IMAGO/Buzzi, Evrim Aydin/Anadolu via Getty Images; **8** Craig Foy/SNS Group/Celtic FC, Jan Kruger – FIFA/FIFA via Getty Images, FIFA, Omar Saaf/FIFA; **9** Franck Fife/AFP via Getty Images, Javier Borrego/Europa Press via Getty Images, Ander Uria/Real Sociedad, Robin Jones – AFC Bournemouth/AFC Bournemouth via Getty Images, AFCB/Amy Maidment; **10** Pat Elmont – UEFA/UEFA via Getty Images, Johnnie Izquierdo/NWSL via Getty Images, Boris Streubel – UEFA/UEFA via Getty Images, David Ramos – UEFA/UEFA via Getty Images, Alex Bierens de Haan – UEFA/UEFA via Getty Images; **11** Alex Davidson – UEFA/UEFA via Getty Images, Alex Bierens de Haan – UEFA/UEFA via Getty Images, Hannah Peters – FIFA/FIFA via Getty Images, Kristy Sparow – UEFA/UEFA via Getty Images, Alex Caparros – UEFA/UEFA via Getty Images; **12** Justin Setterfield/Getty Images, Stuart MacFarlane/Arsenal FC via Getty Images, Stuart MacFarlane/Arsenal FC via Getty Images; **13** Emilee Chinn/Getty Images, Simon Holmes/USSF/Getty Images; **14** Matthew Huang/Icon Sportswire via Getty Images, Robbie Jay Barratt – AMA/Getty Images, Gonzalo Gonzalez/Jam Media/Getty Images; **15** AC Milan/AC Milan via Getty Images, Luca Amedeo Bizzarri – FIGC/FIGC via Getty Images, Abbondanza Scuro Lezzi/EPA/Shutterstock; **16** Jeroen van den Berg/Soccrates/Getty Images, EYE4images/NurPhoto/Shutterstock; **17** Brendon Thorne/Getty Images, Hiroki Watanabe/Getty Images; **18** Stefan Matzke – sampics/Getty Images, Harry Langer/DeFodi Images/DeFodi via Getty Images; **19** Ulrik Pedersen/NurPhoto via Getty Images, Vagelis Georgariou/Action Plus/Shutterstock; **20** Michael Regan – UEFA/UEFA via Getty Images, Laurent Sanson/IMAGO; **21** David Ramirez/Soccrates/Getty Images, Matthieu Mirville/ZUMA Press Wire/Shutterstock, Xinhua/Shutterstock; **22** Chun Yin Ng/Alamy, Maddie Meyer – FIFA/FIFA via Getty Images; **23** Stephane Pillaud/Icon Sport via Getty Images, ProShots/Icon Sport via Getty Images, Brad Smith/ISI Photos/USSF/Getty Images; **24** Ryan Pierse/Getty Images, Roberto Casimiro/SPP/Shutterstock, Paul Phelan/ProSports/Shutterstock; **25** Harry Langer/DeFodi Images/Shutterstock, Matthieu Mirville/ZUMA Press Wire/Shutterstock; **26** Alexandra Fechete/MB Media/Getty Images, Marco Alpozzi/LaPresse/Shutterstock, Ibrahim Ezzat/NurPhoto/Shutterstock; **27** Maciej Rogowski/SOPA Images/LightRocket via Getty Images, Oğuz Yeter/Anadolu via Getty Images; **28** Narong Sangnak/EPA/Shutterstock, IMAGO/GEPA pictures, Cavan Images/Alamy; **29** Lasse Jesper Pedersen/Shutterstock, Gabriele Zampar/Shutterstock, Amazing Aerial/Alamy; **30** Gaspafotos/MB Media/Getty Images, Valery Hache/AFP via Getty Images, Franck Fife/AFP via Getty Images; **31** Immy Thompson-Bland/IPS Photo Agency/Shutterstock, Morgan Hancock/Shutterstock, PA Images/Alamy; **32** Matthew Huang/Icon Sportswire via Getty Images, Matthew Huang/Icon Sportswire via Getty Images; **33** Oscar Del Pozo/AFP via Getty Images, John Sibley/Reuters, Ina Fassbender/Pool/AFP/AFP via Getty Images; **34** Joachim Bywaletz/HMB-Media/IMAGO, Dylan Buell/Getty Images, Kieran McManus/Shutterstock; **35** Dylan Stewart/Image of Sport/Newscom/Alamy, Stephen Brashear/ISI Photos/Getty Images, Daniela Porcelli/ISI Photos/Getty Images; **36** Ryan Pierse/Getty Images, Justin Setterfield/Getty Images, ADIL BENAYACHE/SIPA/Shutterstock; **37** Marvin Ibo Guengoer/Getty Images, IMAGO/CEPix, Christian Kaspar-Bartke/Getty Images for DFB; **38** Jose Breton/NurPhoto/Shutterstock, Harriet Lander – Chelsea FC/Chelsea FC via Getty Images, Alan Edwards/Alamy; **39** Carl Recine/Getty Images, Lexy Ilsley/Manchester City FC, PressFocus/Shutterstock; **40** Neil Hall/EPA-EFE/Shutterstock, Dan Mullan/Getty Images, Alejandro Rios/DeFodi Images via Getty Images; **41** Hugh de Paor/SPP/Shutterstock, Pablo Morano/BSR Agency/Getty Images, Kyle Rivas/Getty Images; **42** Ricardo Nogueira/Sports Press Photo/Getty Images, Manuel Reino Berengui/Defodi Images via Getty Images, Marcelo Endelli/Getty Images; **43** Florencia Tan Jun/Getty Images, Franck Fife/AFP via Getty Images, Matthias Hangst/Getty Images; **44** Yoshikazu Tsuno/AFP via Getty Images, Sepp Hedel; **45** Joe Brady – FIFA/FIFA via Getty Images; **46** Michael Regan/Getty Images for Premier League; **48** Vector Artworks/Shutterstock, Lee Smith/Action Images via Reuters, Paul Marriott/Shutterstock, Lee Parker – CameraSport via Getty Images; **49** BHAFC/Paul Hazlewood, JP Fletcher/Action Plus/Shutterstock, Xinhua/Shutterstock, Andrew Boyers/Action Images via Reuters; **50** ZipDesign/Shutterstock, Florencia Tan Jun/Getty Images, Eric Verhoeven/Soccrates/Getty Images, Javier Soriano/AFP via Getty Images; **51** Ricardo Larreina/Europa Press via Getty Images, Jose Breton/Pics Action/NurPhoto via Getty Images, Juan Manuel Serrano Arce/Getty Images, Alex Caparros/Getty Images; **52** ZipDesign/Shutterstock, Pau Barrena/Bundesliga/Bundesliga Collection via Getty Images, Jan Huebner/IMAGO, Neil Baynes/Getty Images; **53** GSI/Icon Sport via Getty Images, Stefan Matzke – sampics/Getty Images, Marco Steinbrenner/DeFodi Images/DeFodi via Getty Images, Oliver Kaelke/DeFodi Images/DeFodi via Getty Images; **54** ZipDesign/Shutterstock, MB Media/Getty Images, Giuseppe Maffia/NurPhoto via Getty Images, Nicolò Campo/LightRocket via Getty Images; **55** Image Photo Agency/Getty Images, Elianton/Mondadori Portfolio via Getty Images, Jonathan Moscrop/Getty Images, Giuseppe Maffia/NurPhoto via Getty Images; **56** ZipDesign/Shutterstock, Sylvain Thomas/FEP/Icon Sport via Getty Images, Sathire Kelpa/Eurasia Sport Images/Getty Images, Emilian Baldow/Icon Sport via Getty Images, Philippe Lecoeur/FEP/Icon Sport via Getty Images, Jean-Christophe Verhaegen/AFP via Getty Images; **57** Xavier Laine/Getty Images, Jean Catuffe/Getty Images, Mustafa Yalçın/Anadolu via Getty Images, Alex Martin/AFP via Getty Images; **58** ZipDesign/Shutterstock, Shea MacNeil – Vancouver Whitecaps FC/MLS via Getty Images, Frederic J. Brown/AFP via Getty Images, Chandan Khanna/AFP via Getty Images, Peter Joneleit/Icon Sportswire via Getty Images; **59** ZipDesign/Shutterstock, Andre Coelho/EPA/Shutterstock, William Oliveira/Eurasia Sport Images/Sipa US/Alamy, Daniela Xu/Sports Press Photo/SPP/Shutterstock; **60** ZipDesign/Shutterstock, Masashi Hara/Getty Images, Masakazu Senda/GWR, AFLO/Shutterstock; **61** ZipDesign/Shutterstock, Mohammed Saad/Anadolu via Getty Images, Abdullah Ahmed/Getty Images, Stringer/Reuters, Power Sport Images/Shutterstock; **62** ZipDesign/Shutterstock, Melissa Levin/ZUMA Press Wire/Shutterstock, Amanda Loman/NWSL via Getty Images, Howard Smith/ISI Photos/Getty Images, Kyle Rivas/NWSL via Getty Images; **63** ZipDesign/Shutterstock, Harriet Lander – Chelsea FC/Chelsea FC via Getty Images, Immy Thompson-Bland/IPS Photo Agency/Shutterstock, Jess Hornby/Getty Images, Craig Brough/Action Images via Reuters; **64** AlexZaitsev/Shutterstock, Jusanm9102/Dreamstime.com, Gilbert Carrasquillo/GC Images/Getty Images, Michele Nucci/LiveMedia/Shutterstock, Jens Buettner/EPA/Shutterstock, Han Myung-Gu/WireImage, José Sena Goulão/EPA/Shutterstock, BBC/Graeme Hunter/© Hungry Bear Media Ltd; **65** Jusanm9102/Dreamstime.com, Liane Hentscher/HBO, Barry Gossage/NBAE via Getty Images, Ken Lennox/Mirrorpix/Getty Images, BBC Archive, Matt Crossick/Shutterstock for Global; **66** Brendan Moran – Sportsfile/UEFA via Getty Images; **67** Richard Sellers/Sportsphoto/Allstar via Getty Images; **68** Alex Pantling – UEFA/UEFA via Getty Images, Oscar Del Pozo/AFP via Getty Images, Auri Sonea/Icon Sport via Getty Images, Philip Oldham/Shutterstock; **69** Matt Impey/Shutterstock, Richard Sellers/Sportsphoto/Allstar via Getty Images, Giuseppe Maffia/NurPhoto via Getty Images, Marc Atkins/Getty Images; **70** Neville Williams/Aston Villa FC via Getty Images, Romans Koksarovs/IMAGO, Andrej Cukic/EPA/Shutterstock, Zohaib Alam – MUFC/Manchester United via Getty Images; **71** Mikolaj Barbanell/SOPA Images/Shutterstock, George Wood – UEFA/UEFA via Getty Images, Andrzej Iwanczuk/NurPhoto via Getty Images, Kazimierz Koper/IMAGO; **72** Federico Peretti/NurPhoto/Shutterstock, Sipa/Shutterstock, Ricardo Alfieri; **73** Natacha Pisarenko/AFP via Getty Images, Mauricio Duque/Eurasia Sport Images/Getty Images, Marcelo Endelli/Getty Images, Juan Mabromata/AFP via Getty Images; **74** Ahmed Yosri/Reuters, Abdullah Ahmed/IMAGO, Waleed Zein/Anadolu via Getty Images; **75** Power Sport Images/Getty Images, Mohammed Saad/Anadolu via Getty Images, Chine Nouvelle/SIPA/Shutterstock; **76** Hector Vivas/Getty Images, Hector Vivas/LatinContent via Getty Images, Ted S. Warren/Associated Press/Alamy, Francisco Estrada/LatinContent via Getty Images; **77** STR/EPA-EFE/Shutterstock, Siphiwe Sibeko/Reuters, Abeer Ahmed/NurPhoto/Shutterstock; **78** Janerik Henriksson/EPA/Shutterstock, Azra Numanović, Jon Olav Nesvold/Bildbyrån/Shutterstock, David Price/Arsenal FC via Getty Images; **79** Lilou Cassin/Eurasia Sport Images/Getty Images, Glyn Kirk/AFP via Getty Images, Daniela Porcelli/Sports Press Photo/Getty Images, Judit Cartiel – UEFA/UEFA via Getty Images; **80** Federico Peretti/Getty Images, Sebastiao Moreira/EPA/Shutterstock; **81** BackpagePix; **82** Javier Torres/Photosport/IMAGO, Sebastian Frej/IMAGO, Azael Rodriguez/NWSL via Getty Images, Azael Rodriguez/NWSL via Getty Images; **83** Kieran McManus/Shutterstock, Pavel Golovkin/Associated Press/Alamy, Mohamed Tageldin/Middle East Images/AFP via Getty Images, VCG via Getty Images; **84** LightField Studios/Shutterstock, Fedorov Oleksiy/Shutterstock, Jason Mitchell/Headlinephoto Limited/Alamy, Popperfoto via Getty Images, Colorsport/Shutterstock; **85** LightField Studios/Shutterstock, Fedorov Oleksiy/Shutterstock, Jason Mitchell/Headlinephoto Limited/Alamy, The Picture Art Collection/Alamy, Gianni Ferrari/Cover/Getty Images, IMAGO/Buzzi; **86** LightField Studios/Shutterstock, Fedorov Oleksiy/Shutterstock, Jason Mitchell/Headlinephoto Limited/Alamy, Per Pejstrup/Scanpix, Alessandro Sabattini/Getty Images, Alessandro Sabattini/Getty Images; **87** LightField Studios/Shutterstock, Fedorov Oleksiy/Shutterstock, Jason Mitchell/Headlinephoto Limited/Alamy, IMAGO/Buzzi, Gerard Bedeau/Onze/Icon Sport via Getty Images, Michel Barrault/Onze/Icon Sport via Getty Images; **88** LightField Studios/Shutterstock, Fedorov Oleksiy/Shutterstock, Jason Mitchell/Headlinephoto Limited/Alamy, IMAGO/Buzzi, Alain de Martignac/Icon Sport via Getty Images, Alessandro Sabattini/Getty Images; **89** LightField Studios/Shutterstock, Fedorov Oleksiy/Shutterstock, Jason Mitchell/Headlinephoto Limited/Alamy, IMAGO/Buzzi, IMAGO/Laci Perenyi, IMAGO/Buzzi; **90** LightField Studios/Shutterstock, Fedorov Oleksiy/Shutterstock, Jason Mitchell/Headlinephoto Limited/Alamy, Michael Mayhew/Sportsphoto/Allstar via Getty Images, Dal_Zennaro/Shutterstock, Shaun Botterill/Allsport/Getty Images; **91** LightField Studios/Shutterstock, Fedorov Oleksiy/Shutterstock, Jason Mitchell/Headlinephoto Limited/Alamy, Claudio Villa/Allsport/Getty Images, Matthew Impey/Shutterstock, Andrew Cowie/Shutterstock; **92** LightField Studios/Shutterstock, Fedorov Oleksiy/Shutterstock, Jason Mitchell/Headlinephoto Limited/Alamy, Liewig Christian/ABACA/Shutterstock, Elisa Estrada/Real Madrid via Getty Images, Shutterstock; **93** LightField Studios/Shutterstock, Fedorov Oleksiy/Shutterstock, Jason Mitchell/Headlinephoto Limited/Alamy, Shaun Botterill/Getty Images, Cosmin Iftode/Alamy, James Marsh/BPI/Shutterstock; **94** Titus JP/Shutterstock, Filipe Amorim/AFP via Getty Images, Michael Steele/Getty Images, Wang Zhao/AFP via Getty Images; **95** Daily Record/Mirrorpix via Getty Images, PA Images/Alamy, Alain Vartane, James Worsfold/Getty Images; **96** Brendon Thorne/Getty Images; **98** Action Plus Sports Images/Alamy, Jonathan Moscrop/Getty Images, Xinhua/Shutterstock; **99** Ben Radford/Getty Images, Alex Pantling – UEFA/UEFA via Getty Images, Andre Weening/Orange Pictures/Shutterstock; **100** Marvin Ibo Guengoer – GES Sportfoto/Getty Images, Craig Williamson/SNS Group via Getty Images, Fabio Ferrari/LaPresse/Shutterstock, Johanna Säll/Bildbyrån/Shutterstock; **101** Harry Langer/DeFodi Images/DeFodi via Getty Images, Stefan Matzke – sampics/Getty Images, Marius Simensen/Bildbyrån/Shutterstock; **102** Cezaro De Luca/SIPA/Shutterstock, Buda Mendes/Getty Images, William Volcov/Shutterstock; **103** Hector Vivas/Getty Images, Grant Halverson/Getty Images, Cory Knowlton/ZUMA Press Wire/Shutterstock; **104** Tørbjorn Tande/DeFodi Images/DeFodi via Getty Images, Franck Fife/AFP via Getty Images, Christian Liewig/Corbis via Getty Images, Lefty Shivambu/Gallo Images/Getty Images; **105** Abdel Majid Bziouat/AFP via Getty Images, Karim Jaafar/AFP via Getty Images, Paul Ellis/AFP via Getty Images; **106** Saeed Khan/AFP via Getty Images, Xinhua/Shutterstock, Matthew Ashton – AMA/Getty Images; **107** The Asahi Shimbun via Getty Images, Theo Karanikos/AFP via Getty Images, PA Images/Alamy; **108** Patrick Semansky/Associated Press/Alamy Stock Photo, Carlos Ramirez/EPA/Shutterstock, Chandan Khanna/AFP via Getty Images; **109** Bob Thomas Sports Photography via Getty Images, Howard C. Smith/ISIPhotos via ZUMA Wire/Shutterstock, Chandan Khanna/AFP via Getty Images; **110** Jonathan Nackstrand/AFP via Getty Images, dpa picture alliance/Alamy, Harry Langer/DeFodi Images/Shutterstock, Alex Caparros – UEFA/UEFA via Getty Images; **111** Alexander Hassenstein/Getty Images, Michael Zemanek/Shutterstock, Maja Hitij – UEFA/UEFA via Getty Images; **112** AFP via Getty Images, Alex Livesey – FIFA/FIFA via Getty Images, IMAGO/Shengolpixs/Tobi Adepoju, Abdel Majid Bziouat/AFP via Getty Images; **113** IMAGO/Agencia Prensa-Independiente/Henry Lapo, Jose Jacome/EPA/

Shutterstock, Rodrigo Buendia/AFP via Getty Images, Rodrigo Buendia/AFP via Getty Images; **114** Shane Wenzlick/Phototek.nz, Buzzi/IMAGO, Alberto Gardin/Eurasia Sport Images/Getty Images, Oscar Manuel Sanchez/ZUMA Press Wire/Shutterstock; **115** Julio Cesar Aguilar/AFP via Getty Images, Simon Maina/AFP via Getty Images, Caroline Brehman/EPA-EFE/Shutterstock, John Dorton/ISI Photos/USSF/Getty Images for USSF; **116** Doug Pensinger/Getty Images, Adam Pulicicchio/Getty Images; **117** Seb Daly/Sportsfile via Getty Images, José Sena Goulão/EPA-EFE/Shutterstock, David Ramos/Getty Images, Karim Jaafar/AFP via Getty Images, Yasser Al-Zayyat/AFP via Getty Images; **118** Maddie Meyer – FIFA/FIFA via Getty Images; **119** Daniela Porcelli/Eurasia Sport Images/Getty Images; **120** Maja Hitij – FIFA/FIFA via Getty Images, Rico Brouwer/Soccrates/Getty Images, Robert Cianflone/Getty Images; **121** Hannah Peters – FIFA/FIFA via Getty Images, Steph Chambers – FIFA/FIFA via Getty Images, Andrew J. Clark/ISI Photos/ISI Photos via Getty Images, Eric Verhoeven/Soccrates/Getty Images; **122** Luke Hales/Getty Images, Charly Triballeau/AFP via Getty Images, Chris Arjoon/Icon Sportswire via Getty Images, Maja Hitij – FIFA/FIFA via Getty Images; **123** Carl Recine/Getty Images, Image Photo Agency/Getty Images, Alex Pantling – FIFA/FIFA via Getty Images; **124** Darren England/EPA-EFE/Shutterstock, Alex Pantling – FIFA/FIFA via Getty Images, Christophe Saidi/SIPA/Shutterstock; **125** Naomi Baker – FIFA/FIFA via Getty Images, Dennis Grombkowski/Getty Images, Simon Bruty/Sports Illustrated/Getty Images; **126** Marcio Machado/Eurasia Sport Images/Getty Images, Antonio Villalba/Real Madrid via Getty Images, Etsuo Hara/Getty Images; **127** Omar Vega/Getty Images, Jose Breton/NurPhoto/Shutterstock, Franck Robichon/EPA/Shutterstock; **128** Smith Archive/Alamy, Stanley Chou/Getty Images, Francois Nel/Getty Images; **129** Sportimage Ltd/Alamy, Alexandre Schneider/Getty Images, Andrew Cowie/Colorsport/Shutterstock, Johanna Säll/Bildbyrån/Shutterstock; **130** Alex Grimm – FIFA/FIFA via Getty Images; **131** Karim Jaafar/AFP via Getty Images, Harriet Lander – FIFA/FIFA via Getty Images, Aitor Alcalde – FIFA/FIFA via Getty Images, Buda Mendes/Getty Images; **132** Lazyllama/Alamy, Georgi Licovski/EPA-EFE/Shutterstock; **133** Kaz Photography/Getty Images, Shaun Botterill/Getty Images, Victor Fraile/Getty Images, Hector Retamal/AFP via Getty Images, Tomi Hanninen/EPA/Shutterstock; **134** Shaun Botterill – FIFA/FIFA via Getty Images; **136** Stewart Kendall/Sportsphoto/Allstar via Getty Images, National Archives of Poland, AFP via Getty Images; **137** David Cannon/Allsport/Getty Images; **138** IMAGO/BSR Agency, Patrick Hertzog/AFP via Getty Images, IMAGO/Ulmer; **139** Ayman Aref/NurPhoto/Shutterstock, Alex Livesey/Getty Images; **140** IMAGO/Sven Simon, RDB/ullstein bild via Getty Images, Associated Press/Alamy; **141** Offside/L'Equipe, ullstein bild via Getty Images; **142** Michael Steele/Getty Images, Associated Press/Alamy, PA Images/Alamy; **143** Shaun Botterill/FIFA via Getty Images, Gianluigi Guercia/AFP via Getty Images, PA Images/Alamy; **144** Alessandro Sabattini/Getty Images, Brian Bahr/Getty Images, Rolls Press/Popperfoto via Getty Images, Rolls Press/Popperfoto via Getty Images; **145** Jimin Lai/AFP via Getty Images, Gerry Cranham/Offside; **146** Michael Zemanek/BPI/Shutterstock, L'Equipe/Mark Leech Sports Photography/Offside, Colorsport/Shutterstock; **147** Stu Forster/Getty Images, IBL/Shutterstock; **148** Bob Thomas Sports Photography via Getty Images, Popperfoto via Getty Images; **149** AFP via Getty Images, Neil Hall/EPA-EFE/Shutterstock, ZUMA Press Wire/Shutterstock; **150** Mike Egerton/PA Images/Alamy, Vanderlei Almeida/AFP via Getty Images, Mark Leech/Offside via Getty Images, Alain de Martignac/Onze/Icon Sport via Getty Images; **151** Matthias Hangst/Getty Images, Bob Thomas Sports Photography via Getty Images; **152** IMAGO/Agencia MexSport, Newscom/Alamy, Moritz Muller/Alamy; **153** Gerry Cranham/Offside, Simon Stacpoole/Offside/Offside via Getty Images; **154** Sport-Classics/ullstein bild via Getty Images, DPA Picture Alliance/Alamy, Popperfoto via Getty Images, Rolls Press/Popperfoto via Getty Images; **155** DPA Picture Alliance/Alamy, Colorsport/Shutterstock; **156** Keystone/Hulton Archive/Getty Images, Haynes Archive/Popperfoto via Getty Images/Getty Images, Alain de Martignac/Onze/Icon Sport/Icon Sport via Getty Images, 9dream studio/Shutterstock; **157** Achim Scheidemann/EPA/Shutterstock, Associated Press/Alamy, DPA Picture Alliance/Alamy, Georgi Licovski/EPA/Shutterstock, New Africa/Shutterstock; **158** Hector Vivas/Getty Images, Hector Vivas/Getty Images; **160** Igoror/Shutterstock, Damien Chatail; **162** Kara Thomas, Football Association of Wales; **163** Tbcommunication, Football Association of Wales; **164** Paul Michael Hughes/Guinness World Records; **165** Paul Michael Hughes/Guinness World Records; **168** Pedro Porru/MB Media/Getty Images, AFP via Getty Images, David Price/Arsenal FC via Getty Images; **169** Adrian Farias/Getty Images, Alex Livesey/Getty Images, Popperfoto via Getty Images, Kimmo Brandt/EPA-EFE/Shutterstock

COUNTRY CODES

ABW	Aruba
AFG	Afghanistan
AGO	Angola
AIA	Anguilla
ALB	Albania
AND	Andorra
ANT	Netherlands Antilles
ARG	Argentina
ARM	Armenia
ASM	American Samoa
ATG	Antigua and Barbuda
AUS	Australia
AUT	Austria
AZE	Azerbaijan
BDI	Burundi
BEL	Belgium
BEN	Benin
BFA	Burkina Faso
BGD	Bangladesh
BGR	Bulgaria
BHR	Bahrain
BHS	The Bahamas
BIH	Bosnia and Herzegovina
BLR	Belarus
BLZ	Belize
BMU	Bermuda
BOL	Bolivia
BRA	Brazil
BRB	Barbados
BRN	Brunei Darussalam
BTN	Bhutan
BWA	Botswana
CAF	Central African Republic
CAN	Canada
CHE	Switzerland
CHL	Chile
CHN	China
CIV	Côte d'Ivoire
CMR	Cameroon
COD	Congo, DR of the
COG	Congo
COK	Cook Islands
COL	Colombia
COM	Comoros
CPV	Cape Verde
CRI	Costa Rica
CUB	Cuba
CYM	Cayman Islands
CYP	Cyprus
CZE	Czechia
DEU	Germany
DJI	Djibouti
DMA	Dominica
DNK	Denmark
DOM	Dominican Republic
DZA	Algeria
ECU	Ecuador
EGY	Egypt
ENG	England
ERI	Eritrea
ESP	Spain
EST	Estonia
ETH	Ethiopia
FIN	Finland
FJI	Fiji
FRA	France
FSM	Micronesia, Federated States of
GAB	Gabon
GEO	Georgia
GHA	Ghana
GIB	Gibraltar
GIN	Guinea
GMB	Gambia
GNB	Guinea-Bissau
GNQ	Equatorial Guinea
GRC	Greece
GRD	Grenada
GRL	Greenland
GTM	Guatemala
GUM	Guam
GUY	Guyana
HND	Honduras
HRV	Croatia (Hrvatska)
HTI	Haiti
HUN	Hungary
IDN	Indonesia
IND	India
IRL	Ireland
IRN	Iran
IRQ	Iraq
ISL	Iceland
ISR	Israel
ITA	Italy
JAM	Jamaica
JOR	Jordan
JPN	Japan
KAZ	Kazakhstan
KEN	Kenya
KGZ	Kyrgyzstan
KHM	Cambodia
KIR	Kiribati
KNA	Saint Kitts and Nevis
KOR	Korea, Republic of
KWT	Kuwait
LAO	Laos
LBN	Lebanon
LBR	Liberia
LBY	Libya
LCA	Saint Lucia
LIE	Liechtenstein
LKA	Sri Lanka
LSO	Lesotho
LTU	Lithuania
LUX	Luxembourg
LVA	Latvia
MAR	Morocco
MCO	Monaco
MDA	Moldova
MDG	Madagascar
MDV	Maldives
MEX	Mexico
MHL	Marshall Islands
MKD	North Macedonia
MLI	Mali
MLT	Malta
MMR	Myanmar
MNE	Montenegro
MNG	Mongolia
MNP	Northern Mariana Islands
MOZ	Mozambique
MRT	Mauritania
MSR	Montserrat
MUS	Mauritius
MWI	Malawi
MYS	Malaysia
NAM	Namibia
NER	Niger
NGA	Nigeria
NIC	Nicaragua
NIU	Niue
NLD	Netherlands
NOR	Norway
NPL	Nepal
NRU	Nauru
NZ	New Zealand
OMN	Oman
PAK	Pakistan
PAN	Panama
PER	Peru
PHL	Philippines
PLW	Palau
PNG	Papua New Guinea
POL	Poland
PRI	Puerto Rico
PRK	Korea, DPRO
PRT	Portugal
PRY	Paraguay
QAT	Qatar
ROM	Romania
RUS	Russian Federation
RWA	Rwanda
SAU	Saudi Arabia
SDN	Sudan
SEN	Senegal
SGP	Singapore
SHN	Saint Helena
SLB	Solomon Islands
SLE	Sierra Leone
SLV	El Salvador
SMR	San Marino
SOM	Somalia
SRB	Serbia
SSD	South Sudan
STP	São Tomé and Príncipe
SUR	Suriname
SVK	Slovakia
SVN	Slovenia
SWE	Sweden
SWZ	Eswatini
SYC	Seychelles
SYR	Syrian Arab Republic
TCA	Turks and Caicos Islands
TCD	Chad
TGO	Togo
THA	Thailand
TJK	Tajikistan
TKM	Turkmenistan
TMP	East Timor
TON	Tonga
TTO	Trinidad and Tobago
TUN	Tunisia
TUR	Türkiye
TUV	Tuvalu
TZA	Tanzania
UAE	United Arab Emirates
UGA	Uganda
UK	United Kingdom
UKR	Ukraine
UMI	US Minor Islands
URY	Uruguay
USA	United States of America
UZB	Uzbekistan
VAT	Vatican City
VCT	Saint Vincent and the Grenadines
VEN	Venezuela
VGB	Virgin Islands (British)
VIR	Virgin Islands (US)
VNM	Vietnam
VUT	Vanuatu
WLS	Wales
WSM	Samoa
YEM	Yemen
ZAF	South Africa
ZMB	Zambia
ZWE	Zimbabwe

QUIZ ANSWERS

1: Finland (c)
2: Canada (b)
3: Diego Maradona (a)
4: Senegal (c)
5: Arda Güler (b)
6: 10 (c)
7: England (c)
8: Lamine Yamal (b)
9: Australia and France (a)
10: Equatorial Guinea and South Africa (a)
11: Bicycle kick (c)
12: Tottenham Hotspur (b)
13: Kashima Antlers (a)
14: Leeds United (c)
15: Hungary (b)

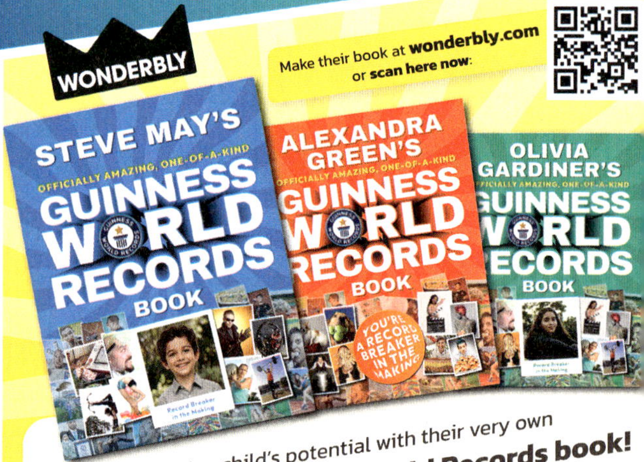

Make their book at **wonderbly.com** or **scan here now**:

Unleash a child's potential with their very own **personalized Guinness World Records book!**

In just a few clicks, create a book spotlighting their name, birthday and interests. They'll see themselves among awesome record breakers and realize they can achieve anything with a bit of curiosity, courage and self-belief.

GWR STORE

RECORD BREAKING AT HOME

EVER PARTICIPATED IN A RECORD ATTEMPT?

Head over to the GWR Store now and grab your official **Record Participant Certificate**!

Sign up now for **10% off** your first order

gwrstore.com